CREATING LEARNING COMMUNITIES:

THE ROLE OF THE TEACHER IN THE 21ST CENTURY

By MARY RENCK JALONGO, Ph.D
Indiana University of Pennsylvania

NATIONAL EDUCATIONAL SERVICE

Bloomington, Indiana • 1991

Copyright © 1991 by National Educational Service
304 West Kirkwood Avenue, Suite 2
Bloomington, Indiana 47404-5132
(812) 336-7700
(800) 733-6786 (toll-free)
FAX: (812) 336-7790
e-mail: nes@nesonline.com
www.nesonline.com

Cover design by Joe LaMantia

Edited by Stanley Elam
Former Editor of *The Kappan*

Printed in the United States of America

Printed on recycled paper

ISBN 1-879639-00-9

This book is dedicated to
the children, college students,
classroom teachers,
administrators, and college
faculty who have taught me
what it means to learn

ACKNOWLEDGEMENTS

SEVERAL PEOPLE played key roles in this project, and I will mention them in order of their involvement. First, I must thank Phil Harris of Phi Delta Kappa International for recommending me as a writer to Alan Blankstein, president of National Educational Service. Nancy Shin of NES supervised this entire project, and it was her wise counsel and cheerful encouragement throughout that brought forth everything that is good in this manuscript. When Nancy told me to "make it fun to read," she freed me to write as a practitioner for fellow practitioners. Also thanks to Nancy, the book had many excellent reviewers whose input improved the manuscript. I owe much to my "in-house" reviewer, my husband Frank. He used his MBA mind and humanistic outlook to examine the logic of my arguments and the reflective power of my words. Thanks, too, to my graduate assistant, Ruth Dunn, who worked patiently and diligently at the library and proofread the finished product.

CONTENTS

PREFACE

DONAL SACKEN (1988) observed that reform literature is almost a cottage industry among professors. "Professor" appears in my title, but this book is not another simplistic call for change from an armchair theorist. I write as a practicing teacher about trusting ourselves as teachers. I follow the lead of Albert Cullum (1971), author of *The Geranium on the Windowsill Just Died But Teacher You Went Right On.* He once told a large group of future teachers that, if he had learned one thing in his career as a teacher, it was "to trust your gut." Albert said that he qualified as an authority on this subject because nearly half of his stomach had been destroyed in the process of discovering that simple truth.

Each day when I am in the schools, working with preservice teachers, inservice teachers, or administrators, I meet people who have been forced or persuaded to go against their professional judgment. Their experiences with children and their reflections on professional practice have moved them beyond mere competence, beyond the requisite knowledge and skills. They have attained a level to which Louis Rubin (1985) refers as "artistry in teaching." It is characterized by decision-making, creativity, perceptivity, and spontaneity. The major frustrations of such outstanding educators is that the attributes of artistry are not nearly as persuasive as a new piece of legislation aimed at school improvement. But legislation does not improve schools; *people* do. This book is about the ways in which the *people* in education can create communities of learning in our schools.

Part One deals with the human side of educational reform and is divided into three chapters: major controversies, authentic learning experiences for children, and creating learning communities. In Part Two, the focus is on teachers as learners, themes and stages in professional development, and issues in the professional development of teachers. The final chapter in Part Two, "Finding Our Voices as Teachers," presents personal narratives — teachers' stories about teaching — which enable each of us to interpret, organize, and guide our professional practice.

I envision this publication as a resource for educators who are ready for gradual, steady, and substantive reform. Effective teachers and administrators will read the recommendations in this book and find validation and support rather than startling revelations. Those who are seeking true innovation will be relieved to find that there are no gimmicks here, no one-word causes for some enterprising staff developer to take on the road. The truth is that reforming schools begins with teachers. Administrators, university faculty, and parents can try to make their jobs easier, but but it is still the teacher who determines the quality of life in a classroom. In today's society, it is often teachers who spend more waking hours with American children than any other adults, including many parents.

This book makes no pretense of having all the answers, but I would like to think that it asks the right questions, the questions that are ignored in political rhetoric and evaded by innovation junkies. We need to recognize that we "have chosen to teach partly *because* teaching is interesting, complicated, perpetually and engagingly problematic" (Editorial Statement, 1990, p. 12). The important issues and the right questions in education are the ones that are identified by teachers. The unit of improvement in American schools is not the nation, the state, the district — not even the school. It is the individual classroom. It is only after we accept this simple truth that we will begin to make headway in school improvement.

Introduction

THIS BOOK is about learning: children's learning, schools and classrooms as learning communities, and teachers as learners. It is based on the following seven premises:

Premise 1: The improvement of education is a human enterprise.

High-quality education results from people working together, not from administrative edict, political rhetoric, or scholarly proposals for reform. Lasting and meaningful educational improvement occurs at the classroom level. The nature of the change required is basically qualitative (how/the process of education) rather than quantitative (how many/the easy-to-measure products of education). In other words, schools will change for the better when teachers are freed to teach in ways that meet students' needs rather than in ways that yield temporary gains in tests composed of low-level multiple-choice items. We have reached the point in education at which our measuring tools have not kept pace with what we know about how children learn. Standardized tests are, at best, one small sample of behavior gathered under very restrictive conditions. At worst, they are used to assess a child's overall learning or a teacher's effectiveness. When they are misused in this way, testing becomes "an anchor against progress" (Goodman, 1982).

Education will become more effective the more we focus on what the ancient Greeks referred to as the *telos,* the overriding purpose that characterizes each profession (Saltis, 1986). In medicine, the guiding principal is to promote health; in law, to administer justice; and, in education, our *telos* has been and must always be to promote learning. The highest purpose of teaching is to promote those types of learning that encourage children to continue to learn, not only inside the classroom but also outside the classroom and throughout life.

In high-quality schools, teachers, administrators, and parents are unswervingly committed to the *telos* of learning. They do not confuse educational means with ends. In a school committed to learning, for example, teachers do not believe that a textbook series (a means) is their program, nor do administrators believe that a test score (another means) should dictate the curriculum.

Premise 2: Authentic learning experiences are the essence of education.

With the notable exceptions of the Progressive Education Movement, Open Education, and Inquiry Learning, behavioristic views of learning have dominated education for decades. In this view, teaching is comparable to filling a tooth. The teacher packs the material in, and if the children are unwilling or the procedure proves painful, they are later rewarded with candy or stickers for their forbearance. Twenty-five years ago, these behavioristic assumptions were practically unquestioned. I can recall being required to take an entire course in "behavior modification." The instructor showed us videotapes of a half-day kindergarten in which children were uncooperative about taking a nap. Then he went in, armed with a bag of miniature marshmallows, and the children were persuaded to pretend to be resting. My question at the time—"Who decided that they need a nap in the first place?"— was clearly unappreciated. Today, educators are asking similar questions about children's learning. Of course, we can condition children to parrot back answers in person or on paper. But, if we dig more deeply, we realize that they lack the underlying concepts; that they are, like the kindergarteners in that videotape, mostly pretending in order to please adults.

The strong challenge to behaviorism is constructivism, the essential element of Piaget's theory (De Vries & Kohlberg, 1990). It looks at learning much differently. Rather than treating knowledge as a disembodied thing that is pressed upon students, constructivism views learning as a process that is individually experienced, constructed, interpreted, and maintained.

Premise 3: High-quality schools and classrooms are learning communities.

Schools change for the better when they stop being bureaucracies and operate more like good families. This is not a platitude; it is the common thread in "America's best-run companies" (Peters & Waterman, 1982), the best model for the education of young children (Silvern, 1988), and the preferred way of fostering growth in literacy (Wells, 1990). Home learning of language is a good model for school learning because it is very organic, spontaneous, interactive, and effective (Moffett, 1981). Those classrooms that are recognized both inside and outside of the institution as extraordinarily effective have embraced the concept of a learning community. The transformation came, not from tinkering with the curriculum guide, but from administrators and teachers trusting one another and working together to make learning the number-one priority.

In the 1990s, it will not be enough for teachers merely to be cooperative, meaning that they get along with their peers, comply with administrative decisions, and avoid confrontation with parents. Teachers in this decade will need to become active collaborators in joint professional efforts that have children's learning as their purpose. As teachers recognize the value of working together, they become increasingly convinced of children's need to work together. Classroom learning communities are the best way to address expanding roles for schools, to get the ballooning curriculum under control, and to meet the needs of an increasingly diverse student population.

Premise 4: Teacher professional development is fundamental to school improvement.

When teachers are asked to identify sources of professional dissatisfaction, their complaints fall into the following categories:

• Low status in the community, lack of recognition, and low salaries

• Inappropriate use of teacher time and talent (such as clerical work or policing the cafeteria)

• Lack of teacher input into curriculum decisions

• Lack of support for instructional problems (such as high student–teacher ratios or inadequate teaching materials)

• Inadequate preparation and support when dealing with special populations of children, such as children with physical disabilities, at-risk children, or gifted students

• Administrative action that assigns teachers to areas outside their interests and competence

• Insufficient opportunities to interact with fellow professionals, especially colleagues (McLaughlin, Pfeifer, Swanson-Owens & Yee, 1986).

Ultimately, teacher professional development must deal with at least some of these issues. Developing professionally is not simply a one-hour or one-day "pep talk" that sends teachers back to the identical conditions without hope for improvement. The very word "development" implies progress. Harriet Jonquiere (1990), who was New York State's 1989 "teacher of the year," says that teachers develop professionally when they learn to "look back," meaning that they keep in touch with their own feelings as children; "look around," meaning that they learn from colleagues and from students; and "look within themselves," meaning that they find the caring and commitment which will make a difference in children's lives.

Premise 5: In order to become resources for one another, teachers need to understand the sequence of teacher professional development.

The difficult adjustment from college student to classroom teacher is a universal experience among teachers. In recent years, theory and research have delineated the many transitions that teachers make throughout their careers, not just at the onset. As educators, we need to understand adult development and teachers' professional development for the same reason that we need to understand child development; both sources of information can help us to explain, predict, modify, and describe behavior. Knowledge of adult and child development can enable us to be more effective in our daily work.

Premise 6: Teachers must use their collective professional judgment and strength to change schools for the better.

When we hear researchers talk about the problem of teacher isolation, we usually envision a teacher with a "closed-door policy" who rarely interacts with another adult. But even teachers who feel as if they are "in a fishbowl," with their skills constantly being scrutinized by visiting teachers, parents, or administrative personnel, may remain isolated. Isolation results, not from the absence of other professionals in the area, but from the lack of opportunity for meaningful professional interaction. Teachers who feel isolated are like the man in a familiar cartoon who, although he lives in a booming metropolis teeming with people, calls out his apartment window: "I'm lonely!" Too often, teachers feel like "a voice in the wilderness" when in fact there are undiscovered kindred spirits and sources of support in the same school or district.

Premise 7: Teachers' personal narratives, their stories, are a rich and virtually untapped resource for learning about learning.

As human beings, we are natural storytellers. Children, almost as soon as they can talk, beg to hear a story. When relatives gather during the holidays, they share family stories. Sometimes, just one teacher's or child's story is like a lightning rod that captures all the energy of its situation, such as *Wally's Stories* (Paley, 1981), *One Child* (Hayden, 1980), *No Place But Here: A Teacher's Vocation in a Rural Community* (Keizer, 1988), or *Among Schoolchildren* (Kidder, 1989). But this appeal of stories is not limited to pleasure reading. In business, stories are scenarios; in law, stories set legal precedents; in psychology or medicine, stories are case studies. In all fields, stories are an important vehicle for reflection, debate, and learning (Dewing, 1954). The stories of teachers are more than interesting anecdotes. The stories that we choose to tell are reflections of our professional perspectives, priorities, and practices. Through the stories of our lives as teachers, we formulate responses to our questions, express our individuality, connect past with present and future, and make the abstract more concrete (Bruner, 1988; Shor & Freire, 1987).

PART ONE

Educational Improvement: A Human Enterprise

Chapter 1

MAJOR CONTROVERSIES IN EDUCATIONAL REFORM

> Many teachers came into the profession inspired by the human good they could do, even as a public service, looking for their students to experience the joy of learning. But now, more than ever, teachers are getting fewer rewards and more distress. They find it harder to celebrate their love of knowledge and devotion to human growth. This is a moment of crisis in the teaching profession.
>
> —Ira Shor, 1987

THE WORD "crisis" has been applied extensively to the field of education. There is a crisis in the classroom, a predicted teacher-shortage crisis, a crisis in teacher education. Crisis is the word we use in America to sound the alarm, and, like a loud bell or buzzer, it commands every person's attention at first, but it does not suggest appropriate action. In fact, there are so many alarms going off that it is sometimes difficult to decide whether we should heed them all. Shor's suggestion that the real crisis in education has to do with the satisfactions of teaching is the one that everyone should heed. We should not disregard this particular alarm, because promoting children's learning is the reason for education's existence. Anything which diverts teachers from that calling is noise.

The Nature of Educational Change

I have a poster in my office that frequently brings comments from visitors. It reads: "It isn't the mountains ahead that wear you down, it's the grain of sand in your shoes." In education, that ever-present grain of sand has to do with trivializing learning and teaching; with oversimplifying educational issues and seeking superficial solutions. We have a reputation for trendiness, for a bandwagon mentality, for latching onto the latest pendulum that swings forward—and, inevitably, backward. Laypersons and those in other professions look at us skeptically because the "latest thing," they feel obligated to remind us, looks more like a revival of the old. When similar objections come from within our own ranks, the teachers who voice them are sometimes labeled malcontents.

Take, for example, one of our buzzwords from the recent past: teacher accountability. In the accountability movement's heyday, most teachers presented the argument that teachers are no more accountable for children's intelligence (defined as a human being's overall capacity for learning) than they are for children's shoe sizes. Even achievement — the child's available storehouse of information on a particular subject, such as reading or math — is only moderately related to one teacher's efforts in a single year. It would stand to reason that the child's knowledge in a given area is an accumulation of previous experiences, not only in all other classrooms but in life in general. Therefore, an individual teacher can take neither the complete credit nor the complete blame for a child's cumulative progress or lack thereof. Learning is developmental and individual. Too many poorly conceptualized "reforms," such as the teacher accountability movement, cause teachers to react to recent trends like sailors on a stormy sea: they wait for it to blow over and go on with the business of teaching. Surrounded by this tumult, is it any wonder that teachers sometimes cling to the one relative constant, the textbook?

FIGURE 1.1
THE CYCLE OF EDUCATIONAL INNOVATIONS

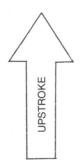

1. Program proposed in the popular press

2. Program piloted without adequate research and development

3. Program introduced in districts with a reputation for innovation

4. Program becomes a "hot topic" among staff developers

5. Rapid expansion of program

6. Controlled evaluations begin

Even before the next "new wave" sweeps over education, some teachers predict its rapid disappearance. They anticipate its exit, not because they wish to sabotage the idea, but because they know what it takes to teach children well. The more opinionated teachers may have expressed their doubts to trusted colleagues out in the hallway and the most assertive ones, right in the meeting which unveiled the Big Idea. This resistance is more than the usual grumbling of employees; it is an insight into the life-cycle of educational innovations, and it is supported by theory and research. Slavin (1989), for example, has described the ebb and flow of educational innovations as consisting of twelve stages. Figure 1.1 is a summary of his description.

This is not to say, of course, that there is no need for change in schools. It is just that the indicators of a need for change and the kinds of solutions which are ultimately proposed are mere window-dressing. Usually, a drop in standardized test scores such as the Scholastic Aptitude Test is taken as proof positive that America is losing the race for international technological and trade superiority. Critics highlight the shocking gaps in students' knowledge base (Bloom, 1987). Then the merry-go-round of blame begins. The public blames the teachers, the teachers blame the administration, and basic education blames higher education for letting so many poor teachers graduate. When educators grow weary of self-blame,

---

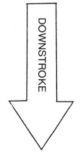

7. Innovative districts move on to other projects

8. Complaints begin to surface

9. Preliminary evaluations are disappointing

10. Developers defend their program, saying that it was poorly implemented

11. Interest in program wanes

12. Results of controlled evaluation studies are published

Source: Adapted from discussion in R. Slavin (1989), "PET and the Pendulum: Faddism in Education and How To Stop It" (*Phi Delta Kappan* 70:752–58)

they begin to blame the parents or, worse yet, the students. Colleges of education deplore the quality of teacher candidates, public education develops a litany of the problems of today's students, and neither takes a problem-solving stance. Instead, these com-

---

FIGURE 1.2
THREE LEVELS OF SCHOOL IMPROVEMENT

	PURPOSE	MAJOR LIMITATION
1. *Pseudo-reform*	To rally support	No effect on professional practice

Examples: Political rhetoric, naming task forces, making superficial changes (e.g., lengthening the school day, assigning more homework), establishing policies with popular appeal (e.g., denying a driver's license to dropouts)

2. *Incremental*	To initiate an innovation for a particular group of children or children within a particular area	Usually dependent on a few optimistic implementers whose enthusiasm wanes in the face of the school bureaucracy; when the implementers move on to the next innovation, change jobs, lose funding or administrative support, project ends

Examples: A grant-supported self-esteem project for children from low-income families, a public school–university research program that uses computer simulations with children in a gifted program

3. *School restructuring*	To completely change the way schools do business	Requires a redefinition of social roles, sharing of power, and is a comparatively slow process

Examples: An authentic "whole language" program, a comprehensive program which restructures the school as a learning community

Source: Adapted from discussion in M. A. Raywid (1990), "The Evolving Effort to Improve Schools: Pseudo-Reform, Incremental Reform, and Restructuring" (*Phi Delta Kappan* 72:139–43).

plaints become a rationalization for failure in education at all levels. This is the sign that we have all hit rock bottom, for we have despaired of our sole purpose for existence: promoting student learning.

Admittedly, every profession does have its members who are incompetent, unethical, or both. But that is reality, not a reason to mistrust everyone, to try to "whip them into shape." If we equate excellence with flawlessness and learning with memorization, teachers learn to play it safe. When teachers feel compelled to teach in ways that contradict their philosophies, their professional development is jeopardized, their creativity suffers, and children's learning is reduced to a high-stakes game of Trivial Pursuit. Functioning in this way is a pale imitation of real teaching. It is as different from real teaching as a paint-by-numbers kit is from an art masterpiece.

What can be done to remedy this situation? First, we must differentiate between meaningful educational reform and other change efforts. The critical difference is implicit in the word "reform," which means to build all over again, to refashion in another image. Actually, reform is the only authentic type of educational change, as Raywid (1990) suggests in Figure 1.2.

What are the real issues in educational reform? Basically, they are the controversies with no simple, one-shot solutions. They are the questions that most politicians evade and most consultants fail to ask. Six issues that I consider to be at the heart of authentic educational reform are discussed below.

Teaching from the Past vs. Education for the Future

Educational philosophers commonly debate whether schools should reflect society as it is or function as agents of change. Actually, schools are rather traditional institutions and have been extremely resistant to change. We can watch a film such as *Dead Poets Society* and, aside from the British setting and the boarding-school formality, see the battles over conformity, control, and tradition that are still being waged today.

Now that the United States is unquestionably a post-industrial society, even that last bastion of tradition, the school, is being assaulted by sweeping societal changes. If we compare the mindset of people who saw themselves putting in 25 years at the factory *versus* the mindset of workers in Silicon Valley, we begin to see how schools must change or become hopelessly out of pace.

Perhaps the most fundamental decision facing American education today is this: Will we prepare our children for the world we remember or the world we can only imagine? As Futrell (1989) points out, some of the administrators, teachers, and parents who affect schools are clinging to an era we have left behind: the industrial era. During America's love affair with manufacturing, it needed people who would follow orders, be satisfied to perform a small task on an assembly line, and persevere to get the gold watch and the retirement benefits.

As society changes, so must our schools change. The decline of the industrial era into the "rust bowl" is as irrevocable as the passing of the horse and buggy. Goodlad (1987) contrasts the ecology of schools yesterday and today as follows:

> The production-factory model justifies all means on the basis of their contributions to predetermined ends . . . The ecological model justifies the functions it performs and the activities it promotes according to their inherent merit—their qualities of goodness (p. 212).

The things that hold the greatest promise for educational reform are those movements with the ecological focus, movements that require fundamental and far-reaching changes in the way that schools do business. Today, I would number cooperative learning and whole language as two such movements. They have captured the imagination of so many teachers, I think, because both trends are affirmations of the learning community.

Covering Material vs. Teaching for Conceptual Change

In the information explosion, the pressure to "cover" everything has become an increasingly insurmountable task for teachers. If we define curriculum as a body of minutiae, the curriculum will continue to snowball with no end in sight. This occurs because school has assumed many educational roles once managed by other institutions. Many schools are dealing with values education, a role once reserved for religious institutions. Many schools are educating students about human sexuality, a role once reserved for families. One thing is clear—the curriculum gets bigger all the time. As one high school teacher put it: "In my career, I've been through the 'new math,' 'hands-on science,' and computers in education, to name a few. Sometimes I feel that it isn't the age on this teacher's body, it's the mileage."

As teachers feel pressured to "cover" more material, children are expected to follow along. Often they do so with even less enthusiasm than weary travelers on a whirlwind tour. How do we break out of this situation? The answer is to stop. Stop covering everything superficially and do fewer things, but do them very well:

> Certainly the material world is too diverse and too complex for anyone to become familiar with all of it in the course of an elementary school career. So the best one can do is to make such knowledge, such familiarity, seem interesting and accessible to the child. That is, one can familiarize children with a few phenomena in such a way as to catch their interest, to let them raise and answer their own questions, to let them realize that what they can do is significant so that they have the interest, the ability and the self-confidence to go on by themselves (Duckworth, 1972, p. 225).

"Coverage" teaching is like being a crew foreman for workers who have to paint a huge building before winter storms hit. The boss assembles all the necessary materials, and it is the boss's job to keep the workers on task. They hurry along, wanting nothing more than to get it over with. Excellence is out of the question. The goal is to slap on paint and cover as much area as possible each day. The best they can hope for is to keep the structure from deteriorating further. In teaching, an emphasis on coverage is equally frustrating for teachers and students. Everyone honestly feels that it is boring, and only a small percentage of teachers and students will persist with any measure of enthusiasm.

A good analogy for teaching children to *dis*cover is supporting them as they create a mural. We note each child's progress while watching the larger image take shape. We organize materials, ask questions, make suggestions, stop to admire quality work, and encourage cooperation. But we do not take control of the child's brush and paint for him or her because we understand that the mural belongs to the children. Coaching, in the most positive sense of that word, characterizes our interactions with children. We become students of our students, noting how their purposes and techniques evolve and thinking about what would enable each child to move on to other levels or in other directions. The children are motivated by their desire to produce something of quality, something remarkable. This type of teaching is satisfying for children and adults because it allows both to attain at the highest levels of which they are capable. William Glasser (1990) explains how this occurs:

Most competent teachers recognize . . . that the effort to stuff students with measurable fragments of knowledge has little or nothing to do with high-quality education. For competent teachers, it has become a miserable Catch-22. If they teach conceptually and challenge students to think and defend their ideas, the students will have a chance to learn something worthwhile. But, since the students may not do well on tests that measure fragments, such teachers will be labeled as trouble-makers and failures. On the other hand, if they teach the way they are told to teach, the students will fail to learn anything that the students believe is worthwhile. But their teachers will be praised as successful team players, and the students will be blamed as incompetent. There is always the fear in education, especially among the measurers and fragmenters, that too great a concern with quality means that students inevitably cover less ground. The opposite occurs; quality always leads to increased productivity (p. 430).

Teachers as Technicians vs. Teachers as Decision-Makers

The driving force behind curriculum should be theory, research, and collective professional judgment. Too many teachers have had a "teacher-proof" curriculum foisted upon them. These materials are unabashedly designed to promote mediocrity, the assumption being that even the worst teachers can "cover" the basic content by doing exactly as the developers recommend. Too often, those prepackaged materials, which are really used to bring incompetents into compliance, end up hindering the expert teachers from doing their best (Jalongo, 1986). This occurs whenever administrators interpret fair treatment as identical treatment and insist that every teacher follow the teacher's manual. Or, worse yet, they enforce unenlightened policies such as "every child must complete every workbook page" or "a child cannot progress to the next grade level unless he or she has read every book in the reading series." Ultimately, dependence upon prepackaged curricula prevents teachers from teaching in ways that are satisfying. As Sykes (1983) observes, "routinized instruction and the attendant loss of autonomy makes teaching unpalatable for bright, independent-minded college graduates and fails to stimulate the pursuit of excellence among those who do enter. Over the long run, the routinization of instruction tends to deprofessionalize teaching" (p. 120).

Minimum Competency Testing vs. Education for Excellence

Harold Howe (1983), former United States Commissioner of Education, put the testing mania in perspective when he suggested that evaluating the quality of schools by test scores alone is like judging a congregation by the amount of money in the collection plate: it tells you something, but it will not tell you much. He further recommended that the politicians who deplore children's scores on these tests be required to take the tests themselves and then publish the results. Linda Darling-Hammond (1984) compares education's singleminded focus on testing to an imaginary medical profession that concerns itself exclusively with the patient's temperature rather than with overall health; the patient dies, but his temperature stays down. An issue of *Harper's Magazine* (1986) took the medical analogy one step further, noting that: "The reforms, aimed at an already heavily bureaucratic and inflexible system, propose to heal the patient by administering more of what made him sick" (p. 39).

The major flaw in a hard-line minimum-competency testing program is one that any layperson could identify: What about the child whose intellectual abilities prevent him or her from achieving high school levels of proficiency? Surely, there is much to be said for having high expectations for students. But reality would dictate that, despite some children's and teachers' best efforts, some children will remain unable to meet even minimum standards for performance. The quality-control procedure of an appliance manufacturer simply does not translate well in the dynamic, human enterprise of education.

The whole concept of minimum competency is even shakier if we accept Gardner's (1983) contention that there are seven types of intelligence — logical–mathematical, linguistic, spatial, kinesthetic, musical, interpersonal, and intrapersonal. What type of paper-and-pencil test could we envision that would even begin to assess growth in each of these areas? The fundamental dilemma is simply this: Do we force the child to fit an inflexible, hierarchical, age-determined, and traditional structure, or do we shape the schools to meet the needs of students?

Product Orientation vs. People Orientation

Far too many educational ideas derive from the requirements of managing things or animals rather than people (Glasser, 1990). Behavioral objectives did not originate with people management but with materials management. Most of the systems used to evaluate schools are based on antiquated factory assembly-line management assumptions (Callahan, 1962). If, as Paulo Freire (1972) contends, oppression is any act that prevents us from becoming more fully human, then these efficiency-expert assumptions are oppressing teachers. Schools remain impervious to change because of tradition, because of an over-reliance on textbooks, because of abuses of standardized testing, and because most change efforts rarely move beyond a fifty-minute segment of the teacher's time (Eisner, 1990). Single-issue solutions simply do not have the power to shake the pillars of bureaucracy that undergird much of public education. Change will come when we focus on teachers in a comprehensive way:

> Clearly, just increasing teachers' salaries will not alter the basic conditions that prevent teachers from teaching. Just decreasing class sizes will not keep effective teachers from leaving the profession, if they continually confront parental apathy or intrusion. Just increasing opportunities for professional development will do little to make teachers effective, if a building administrator fails to protect them from unnecessary interruptions and paperwork or fails to manage the school in a fashion that supports instructional efforts. A comprehensive agenda of reform is necessary to structure the teaching profession for success (McLaughlin, Pfeifer, Swanson-Owens & Yee, 1986).

The Quest for Panaceas vs. Exploring Options

There were nods of agreement all around when I told a group of teachers that the real source of teacher "burnout" is teaching in a way that contradicts your philosophy or being launched into one innovation after another. Even though we do not have religion in public schools, innovations are sometimes pursued with religious fervor. Take, for example, the "process approach to writing" movement. Although this trend has much to recommend it, it is not an article of faith. As one teacher put it: "I know Donald Graves would shudder, but why is it so terrible for a teacher to take dictation for a reluctant writer? I know that it is supposed to take away the child's 'ownership' of the piece of writing, but where does that leave a voice-activated computer program that enables children to speak and have their words appear in print? And I know that you aren't supposed to use story starters or tell children how to spell words. But it seems to me that if you're careful not to overdo it, any of these things could be useful under certain conditions with a particular child."

Until we begin to look at new ideas as part of a repertoire, a range of options, we will fail to make the type of "steady, widely acknowledged and irreversible progress" that characterizes other fields such as agriculture or engineering (Slavin, 1989). The expert in agriculture knows that higher crop yields and ecological responsibility must be balanced. The engineer knows that structural integrity and cost-effectiveness must be preserved. These professions know that other considerations are subordinate to these fundamental goals. In education, the irrefutable goal is promoting lifelong learning and respecting learners. The best teachers do this already, even though the system usually rewards those who treat the child as a disembodied intellect. Until teachers are supported in their efforts to educate the "whole child"—physical, social, emotional, and intellectual—we will fail to make the kind of progress we seek.

Chapter 2

PROVIDING AUTHENTIC
LEARNING EXPERIENCES FOR CHILDREN

The problem of education is to help the pupil see the forest by means of the trees.   —Edgar Dale, 1984

That's what education means, to be able to do what you've never done before.   —Alice Freeman Palmer, 1984

WHAT IS LEARNING? Psychologists usually define learning behaviorally; that is, as a change in behavior. But this definition works much better with observable skills-in-action (such as driving a car) than it does with insights-in-action (such as visionary leadership). Glasser (1990) challenges the behavioristic view of learning when he says:

> What happens outside of ourselves has a lot to do with what we choose to do, but the outside event does not cause our behavior. What we get—and all we ever get—from the outside is information. How we choose to act on this information is up to us. [S]tudents are the ones who make the final judgment on how important they think the information is to them. The more important they think the information is, the more they will do what they are asked, and the better they will do it (p. 432).

A Constructivist Perspective

In recent years, many of our assumptions about learning have been challenged by Piaget's theory of constructivism. Kamii (1988) explains constructivism as follows:

> Children acquire knowledge by creating one level after another of being "wrong," rather than by internalizing correct, adult knowledge from the beginning. The most obvious example of

the constructive process is young children learning to talk. They do not speak in complete sentences from the beginning. [C]hildren create their own knowledge out of what they experience in the environment. These "wrong" ideas are necessary steps in children's construction of increasingly higher levels of knowledge (p. 182).

In fact, no matter how tightly controlled our written, taught, and tested curriculum becomes, there will always be two uncontrolled variables: the teacher's interpretation of that curriculum and the curriculum as it is experienced by the child (Rogers, 1989). Take, for example, two teachers who are ostensibly teaching a unit about China. Both follow the curriculum guide, both groups of students will use the same study guide, both classes will be evaluated with the same test. But the first teacher reinforces stereotypes with an "Aren't these people strange?" attitude, while the second teaches the children about China from a multicultural perspective, emphasizing both uniqueness and similarities.

Even if the second teacher taught both classes, the curriculum would differ for each child, depending upon such things as the child's prior knowledge, level of interest, ability to focus, and so forth. Emig (1981) explains it this way:

That teachers teach and children learn no one will deny. But to believe that children learn because teachers teach and only when teachers teach is to engage in magical thinking . . . from a developmental point of view (p. 21).

Redefining Learning

The great fallacy of educational experiments designed to compare one teaching method with another is to believe that we can, like an agriculturist, control all the variables save one and attribute differences in growth to that one variable. The researcher in agriculture can analyze the soil and make the plots of ground equal to begin with; the most that an educational experimenter can do is randomly select and assign. The agriculturist can quantify the number of hours of sunlight, measure the amount of rainfall, monitor every environmental condition; educational experimenters find it difficult to train teachers to use specific methods equally well, to assess the influence of teacher personality on children's learning, or to describe the interactions between teacher and method. Teachers' effects on children's learning are less like a crop-yield

FIGURE 2.1
CONTRASTING VIEWS OF EDUCATION

"Back to Basics" View	*Constructivist View*
Knowledge dispensed by teacher and absorbed by learner	Knowledge is constructed through reflection, inquiry, and action
Knowledge is permanent, crystallized	Knowledge is temporary, fluid
Knowledge is objective, a body of facts	Knowledge is subjective, self-discovered, and interpreted

Source: Adapted from discussion in C. T. Fosnot (1989), *Enquiring Teachers, Enquiring Learners: A Constructivist Approach* (New York: Teachers College Press).

experiment and more like the real-life farmer's situation. The successful farmer does everything in his or her power to promote growth but has to face the elements every day. Plants do not flourish because we wish them to or tell them to. They flourish because we create optimal conditions for them to grow themselves. Children's learning works much the same way because learning is an inside-out operation (Hoffman & Lamme, 1989). Figure 2.1 contrasts the "back to basics" behavioral view of learning with a constructivist orientation.

Characteristics of Authentic Learning Experiences

Following an extensive review of the research on learning, Langer and Applebee (1986) identified these five features of authentic learning experiences:

1. *Ownership.* Both children and teachers assume greater responsibility for their own learning. Learning is personal and emulative.

2. *Appropriateness.* The learning activities are shaped to the needs of the learners rather than the other way around.

3. *Structure.* There are structures and routines, but they are not "carved in stone." The structure is more implicit than explicit (i.e., evident in the environment and organization of activities rather than in a predetermined response from the child).

4. *Collaboration.* Children are involved in a variety of flexible

groups, work with same-age and cross-age partners or tutors, work with larger groups (such as presentations to the entire class or school), work with members of the larger community.

5. *Internalization*. What children learn is truly part of them because they have been actively involved throughout. Internalization rarely occurs in depersonalized classrooms in which whatever the children "are as people gets dropped by the door as they come in and picked up again as they leave" (Eisner, 1988, p. 524).

As these five characteristics suggest, we need to abandon the idea that knowledge is bestowed upon children by adults, that children are passive recipients of adults' ready-made solutions. Educators in the field of aesthetics have a motto that all teachers should take to heart: "There is nothing worth doing that isn't worth doing badly at first." Perhaps the most important question that teachers can ask is: How do children learn? One way to gain some perspective is to look within ourselves. Reflect for a few moments on your most and least successful learning experiences. Describe them. What made one experience satisfying and the other so frustrating? Here is how one teacher used her experience of learning to bake bread as a metaphor for learning:

> I realized I had had demonstrations of bread making from my mother, the home economics teacher, and from the authors of the books I used to help me understand the process. I had encouragement from my husband and friends. I had initiated the interest and had a desire to learn. The results of my repeated attempts were accepted and helped me gain confidence in my bread-making ability. But more than that, I was in control of the learning situation; I decided when I was ready to try something unfamiliar or difficult (Bent, 1990, p. 57).

The challenge of education is to take those keys to success in learning—the demonstrations, the material resources, the supportive climate, and the individualization—and implement them in a classroom full of children.

Children as Learners

To begin this look at how children learn, consider these behaviors of three kindergarten children:

Melissa writes a letter to her father who is on a business trip. At the end of her letter she writes:

Do you love me?

YES   NO

(Circle one)

Roberto is visiting his grandmother and the radio is on. When a test of the Emergency Broadcast System is announced, he stops and listens. "They keep saying it's a test," he says with a tone of exasperation, "but they never ask any questions!"

Rhianna is eating her cereal and looking out on a wintry landscape when her mother informs her that she has the day off—a snow day. Instead of rejoicing, Rhianna looks grave and says, "Mom, you just don't know how many papers I'll have to make up."

All of these five-year-olds are telling us something about the way they have been socialized into formal education. Melissa applies the yes/no response format, even to complex emotions, just as we apply the multiple-choice format to measures of academic progress. Roberto waits to be evaluated, just as teachers and schools await the results of the Iowa Test of Basic Skills or the California Achievement Tests. Rhianna already knows what it is like to be deluged by paperwork, as so many teachers and administrators are. All three of these children are highly successful in school, but what impression do they have of learning? And what about the children who are not nearly as talented at doing schoolwork? What are their impressions of learning? Perhaps they have concluded, as one unhappy first-grader put it, "Just do your papers and get as many stars as you can." If they have learned this lesson from their lessons, the consequences are serious, not only for learning today, but also for learning throughout life. These children believe that learning is something to be endured; something that is initiated, controlled, and rewarded outside of themselves; something with little value outside the walls of the schoolhouse.

Now think about a childhood passion, something that you learned without being pressured by adults. Chances are, it could be characterized as follows:

• You initiated the learning experience and were motivated to pursue a goal

• You selected goals and obstacles that you perceived as neither too easy nor too difficult. You considered various routes to achieving the goal and selected those that you considered most appealing, based on your knowledge of yourself

• You sought models to emulate and looked for other sources of information

• You received encouragement and used your mistakes as opportunities for learning

• You paced yourself and decided when you were ready to move on

But do our classrooms reflect these characteristics? If they do not, then they are not learning communities and the *telos* of learning is circumspect. The two adages that much of what children learn is "better caught than taught" and that "teaching is more than telling" are more than conventional wisdom. They are clearly supported by learning theory.

Four Types of Learning

Recently, I was invited to speak to a group of teachers at their unified inservice day on the topic of "whole language." One key controversy surrounding this approach to literacy development can be summarized as follows: Do we see children's language-learning as something that moves from part to whole (from letters to words to sentences), or do we believe that children acquire literacy from whole to part (begin with enjoyment of stories and gradually learn to use word-analysis skills)? The question that I posed to teachers that day was simply this: Many of you are parents or know some young language learners very well; how would you describe their book behaviors? These teachers described the toddlers they knew pointing to and commenting upon the pictures in books, pre-schoolers memorizing favorite books, asking to hear the same story repeated, pretending to read, and asking questions about printed material. In fact, nearly every behavior they described in children before they were "officially" taught to read supported a "whole language" theory. I then asked them to estimate the average number of books read annually by an adult. Most said three or four or five; the statistics suggest less than one. We looked briefly at illiteracy statistics, which are sufficiently shocking in themselves. Then we looked at some of the facts about *aliteracy,* people who know how to read but choose not to. We discussed, for example, the fact that, in America, eighty percent of all books published are read by ten percent of the population.

The question in children's literacy learning, then, is not, "Can we teach children 'basic skills'?" The question is, "What happens in

the long run?" What would we think of a dance studio whose
students disliked dancing, even quit dancing at the first opportunity?
And what about children? What do they say? I shared Doris
Roettger's (1978) study with the group. Roettger asked children
how to improve reading instruction, and their responses could be
categorized as follows:

1. Children should be given a chance to read every day.

2. Teachers should ask them about their interests and help
children find books on the subject.

3. Teachers should recommend good books and talk about
them.

4. Children should have opportunities to talk about favorite
books with each other and with the teacher.

When my language-arts classes interviewed children using the
same questions, they obtained similar answers. Children want
literature, not workbooks and ditto sheets. In fact, many children
differentiated between "real reading" (as in library books) and
"boring reading" (as in reading class).

As the interview suggests, there is much more to reading than
decoding words. In fact, children can easily become expert decoders
who fail to comprehend what they read or dislike reading. Lilian
Katz (1988) describes a way of conceptualizing children's learning
that is especially useful. She identifies four types of learning:

• *Knowledge,* which is information children get through their
senses, from experience

• *Skills,* which are developed through practice

• *Dispositions,* which arc "habits of mind" such as curiosity
and are learned from role models

• *Feelings,* which are the emotions associated with the learning
experience.

A metaphor for this conceptualization of learning is an iceberg.
Knowledge and skills are obvious and above the surface, but the
bulk is concealed below. When we teach children knowledge and
skills without attention to dispositions, we know what happens.
Children get the message, "Do as I say, not as I do." In an interesting analysis of highly successful reading programs, Hallinger and
Murphy (1985) emphasized how important it was for adults to
model the desired behavior. They described one school where for
fifteen minutes after lunch, everyone, including the janitor, dropped
everything and read. This is a good illustration of an effort to
influence children's "habits of mind" by providing role models. But
even providing models for children to emulate is not enough. If we

teach without any attention to children's feelings, we deny their personhood.

In a classroom with a constructivist philosophy, one that teaches for conceptual change, we find children absorbed in authentic learning experiences. Take, for example, a science lesson described by Watson and Konicek (1990). Fourth-grade students have expressed the opinion that winter hats, gloves, sweaters, and the like give off heat. Rather than telling them that this is not so, the teacher invites the children to experiment. They place thermometers inside several objects that they believe will generate heat, then leave them overnight. When the thermometers do not rise, the children conclude that somehow cold air has gotten inside. The children use several techniques to keep the objects from being chilled by the surrounding air, such as sealing them in plastic bags, in closets, or inside a down sleeping bag. Throughout these and later experiments:

- The children are engaging directly with a phenomenon
- The children are making and recording observations
- The teacher is helping children to see the relevance between their prior experiences and the phenomenon under study
- The teacher is encouraging children to make predictions and test their assumptions
- The teacher stresses consistency, asking children to consider how contradictory statements can both be true
- The children are learning to note discrepancies, to propose understanding and plausible explanations, and to engage in further testing and observation (Duckworth, 1986; Watson & Konicek, 1990)

Clearly, this type of teaching proceeds more slowly and appears less well organized to the casual observer. But, if we move at a rapid pace in a lockstep curriculum, we are missing the meaning. I am reminded of a battered curriculum chart that was posted on the inside of my classroom door during my early years of teaching. It was the well-organized product of several adult minds from the State Department of Education. The neat squares delineated what content should be taught at each grade level. Before I started to teach, the chart seemed rather reassuring. I knew, for example, that I had to teach cursive writing, a unit on solid and liquid measurement, a social studies unit on "families around the world." But then the children arrived. The majority of them were desperately poor. Estrella, using her very best handwriting, wrote and illustrated a story about how her teeth "rawted out"; they were blackened stumps so badly abcessed that she could barely talk or keep food down. During the unit on measurement, we made no-bake cookies, and Hector confided that he did not have "cooked stuff because the stove was broke"; to add credence to this claim, his mother sent me a note the next day asking for the recipe, then sent me an effusive thank-you note which implied that they had been without a stove for quite some time. A shy little redhead named Eddie, who was a long-term substitute teacher's son, was one of the few who did not qualify for free lunches; when his single-parent mother went on a job interview to a neighboring state, she was killed in a car crash. I decided to skip my happy textbook unit on the nuclear family. The nurse and I found a dentist for Estrella. Another teacher donated a used stove to Hector's family. When I arrived at school each day, Eddie was standing outside, waiting for the doors to open, and his grandmother and I agreed to let him come early and stay late; we needed that time together. I tore the chart down.

Individualization Revisited: The Project Approach

Ask any teacher to describe an ideal classroom, and he or she is apt to mention meeting individual needs. Where individualization for children is concerned, the common misconception is that it means preparing a separate packet of papers for each child in the class. Then, because teachers have so many students, the whole idea is abandoned as being too complex. Actually, individualization is much simpler than that. The secret is to individualize by providing options. Take, for example, the high school history teacher whose content is the Civil War. He can use the traditional approach of lecturing while his students take notes, testing them later on the memory of the material. Or he can individualize, giving an open-ended assignment and beginning with questions such as these:

What do you already know about the Civil War?

What questions do you have?

How can we efficiently organize to find answers to our questions and verify what we know?

Basically, the students know that the Civil War was also called the War Between the States, that it had to do with slavery, that Lincoln was President, and that there were great sacrifices on both sides. Laura asks how much of *Gone With the Wind* and *The Andersonville Trial* was historically accurate. Eiho wants to know why the differences between North and South could not be resolved. Some other questions from students:

What weapons and artillery were used?

Was Manassas (the local battlefield) considered an important battle?

Can we go on a field trip?

Can we watch the PBS miniseries on the Civil War?

Can we make our own videotape?

Organizing further study, the children decide to form interest groups in order to focus on different topics such as clothing and uniforms, foods, social customs, battles and generals, spies and and espionage, slavery and slaves, music and dance, art and photography, and field-trip preparation. They also decide to communicate with others by producing a Civil War videotape using photographs from books, personal narratives from published sources, authentic music, a poster/timeline of the key events, and original drawings of costumes and uniforms.

This project approach to achieving greater individualization is currently undergoing a revival (see Glover, 1990; Katz & Chard, 1985). The project method was originally proposed by Kilpatrick in 1918 and is already in wide use in gifted and talented programs. Perhaps you have heard of a class going on a simulated archeological dig in which they learn about an imaginary culture from its artifacts. This activity qualifies as a project because:

• It incorporates all of the subject areas and helps children to see the interrelatedness of knowledge

• It meets children's needs for social interaction and builds interpersonal skills

• It enables children to work to their strengths and allows every child to make a contribution

• It allows children to become fully involved in an in-depth investigation

• It convinces children that they can do high-quality work

• It makes children aware of the contributions of other cultures and points of view

• It forges connections with the larger community

Although the project method has much to recommend it, it too is more of a philosophy than a technique. As Webster (1990) points out, teachers who involve children in projects need to ask:

Which projects for which children?

What do children already know?

What meaningful learning is possible for children within a project?

What resources, attitudes, questions should be brought in?

What features of the child's involvement can reveal growth? How can this growth be assessed?

Authentic learning experiences, individualization, and the project approach come very close, I believe, to what is meant by talk about educational excellence. Recently, a group of inservice teachers reconfirmed my belief. Rather than assigning them the lecture plus discussion plus "research" paper formula, I told them that I wanted them to create two major projects in their classrooms that met three requirements. First, the projects would reflect state-of-the-art research and teaching methods; second, the projects would be developmentally appropriate and allow every child to experience success; and finally, the projects would be something that they as classroom teachers would be thrilled about and proud to share with one another. When the students wanted to know the minimums—how many pages, the number of references, and the duration of the project—I simply said: "Surprise me. Dazzle us. I will meet with you individually to give you guidance." I was surprised, and we were dazzled. A special-education teacher hatched ducks with her high school students during a unit on life-cycles, and they created a chart-sized, illustrated book of their observations, which they presented and donated to a kindergarten class. A middle school teacher did a unit on the elderly, and his students corresponded with and visited their pen pals at a nearby residential facility for the aged. A remedial-reading teacher replaced phonics drill with a literature-based curriculum, and one of her second-grade nonreaders blossomed into a reader in a semester's time.

The stories that these teachers told about teaching in this way sometimes brought tears of empathy, sometimes peals of laughter and fun-filled banter, and sometimes the gooseflesh of insight and inspiration. In every case, members of the class were reawakened to the joys of teaching. Whenever I see them, they always say that it was their best graduate education experience. They say how much they learned from one another and how they continue to use what they have learned. Ironically, I "taught" less and "covered" less, but the students learned more. It took teachers to teach me what the ancient philosopher Comenius meant when he said that it is the teacher's challenge "to seek and find a method whereby teachers teach less and learners learn more."

Chapter 3

CREATING AND SUSTAINING
LEARNING COMMUNITIES

Decades of research and reform have not altered the fundamental
facts of teaching. The task of universal, public, elementary education is still usually being conducted by a woman alone in a little
room, presiding over a youthful distillate of a town or city. If she
is willing, she tries to cultivate the minds of children in both good
and desperate shape. Some of them have problems that she hasn't
even been trained to identify. She feels her way. She has no choice.
— Tracy Kidder, 1989

IN ORDER for schools to improve, the structure of the world which
Kidder describes must change. Human beings' basic needs for
quality of life in a social group suggest the direction of those
changes. Both children and adults have five basic needs: survival,
love, power, fun, and freedom (Glasser, 1989). Too often, schools
treat learning as if it were a simple act of cognition when it clearly
has complex psychological, sociological, and political aspects. If
we look into the classrooms where children are learning well, we see
how teachers address and balance children's needs. Good teachers
do not resort to a grim "You'll thank me someday" mentality; they
make learning important here and now. Good teachers do not
follow outmoded stereotypes about teacher behavior; they teach as
they would want their own children to be taught. One of the
hallmarks of high-quality education is that teachers believe they
can do something for every child. As a result, the learners are given
a sense of their own powers — the power to think, to express ideas in
many forms, to accept rather than resist growth. In America's finest
classrooms, there is structure and routine, but there is also freedom.
Teachers have the autonomy to teach in ways that meet children's
needs, while children learn to make responsible choices about their
own learning.

Open System and Closed System Assumptions

Thinking of the school as a system — open or closed — helps us to understand why one-dimensional solutions do not improve schools and teaching. Most people approach the task of school improvement simplistically: institute a health and wellness program or raise salaries or involve teachers in decision-making or form partnerships with the community or . . . or, but never and . . . and . . . Arthur Combs (1988) contends that educational reform efforts fail because we treat schools as closed systems rather than open systems. Figure 3.1 highlights what happens when we make the closed-system assumptions.

FIGURE 3.1
OPEN VS. CLOSED SYSTEMS

Closed systems work best when:	*Open systems work best when:*
The focus is on things	The focus is on people
Goals are clear and simple	Objectives are broad and complex
The leader controls goals and can predict outcomes	The outcomes cannot be predicted and control must be shared

Source: A. Combs (1988), "New Assumptions for Educational Reform" (*Educational Leadership* 45:38–40).

Barriers to Learning Communities

As I observe in a first-grade classroom, the day begins with a child using a pointer and leading the children in a chant of all the letters of the alphabet and their corresponding sounds. The teacher sits at her desk, taking attendance and the lunch count. When the first-graders get restless, she leaves her desk and begins with a lesson on manners. The topic today is how to behave on a date. The teacher chooses children (mostly those who have been misbehaving) to enact various situations (such as greeting the person at the door, responding appreciatively to a gift of flowers, being seated at a restaurant table) while the rest of the class roars with laughter whenever the teacher criticizes a child's response. After these opening exercises, she introduces me, and the children greet me in unison. "Oleta," the teacher commands, "take your writing folder over to our visitor and let her read it. Oleta is one of our best writers."

Unlike most of the other children in this class, Oleta is dressed as if she were going to church. Her hair is beaded and braided, her dress frilly and fashionable, and her shoes are patent-leather, shiny and impractical. She approaches me timidly and hands me the folder. Inside are samples of painstaking printing and virtually flawless spelling. Any errors that have been made are circled in red by the teacher, and the correct spellings are printed neatly above. My impression from Oleta's writing is that she is an economically advantaged child in a community where most families are economically disadvantaged. She writes about singing songs with her mother, who plays the guitar professionally. She also describes a family vacation at Disney World. I find a slip of paper and write her a thank-you note. The morning drags on with phonics workbook pages, basal reading lessons, and timed mathematics problems on ditto sheets. When I visit the teachers' lounge, teachers are grousing about a mandatory meeting later in the week. The new superintendent has begun publishing the average test score from each teacher's class, and it has created quite a furor. They tell me that these children are difficult, some of them unsalvageable. They give me all of the reasons why they cannot succeed; a few try to shock me with favorite horror stories about the children's lives.

This scenario illustrates what happens when learning communities become dysfunctional. Everyone feels threatened and mistrusted, and a power struggle ensues. There are low expectations all around, and nobody can see the way out of a desperate situation.

> [P]hysically, barriers exist in lack of resources and equipment; administratively, in regulations and procedures; philosophically, in differing opinions about desirable goals and objectives, and psychologically, in personal feelings, attitudes and beliefs (Combs, 1988, p. 40).

Remember the film *Stand and Deliver*? Escalante faced the physical barrier of no computers for his computer class. He faced philosophical and administrative barriers by being at odds with the policies and beliefs of his colleagues. In the movie, the school is in jeopardy of losing its accreditation and everyone is deploring the situation when Jaime Escalante says quietly, "Students will rise to the expectations of their teachers." His story is remarkable for the same reason that a trapeze artist performing without a net is impressive — he endangers himself by working without support. He creates a learning community within the confines of his classroom through monumental self-sacrifice.

In a dysfunctional learning community, teachers have three choices: fight, disengagement, or flight. Some courageous teachers fight, either openly as Escalante did, or by shutting out the world of school beyond their classroom walls. Still others become apathetic and distance themselves from the students; they begin to view the children as personified drains on their physical stamina and emotional stability; they struggle to keep their classrooms running in neutral, avoiding high or low gear. Other teachers leave the profession entirely. It is easy to understand why an unsuccessful teacher would leave the profession, but why do good teachers leave teaching? I think that it is because, as Sizer (1985) once remarked:

> Excellent teachers are strong, proud people. Strong, proud people only take jobs which entrust them with important things and which are structured in such a way that success is reasonably possible (p. 424).

Trist (1976) contends that the expectations of workers in contemporary society are in transition. Employee expectations have moved from independence to interdependence, from self-control to self-expression, from achievement to self-actualization, and from endurance of distress to capacity for joy. Unless teachers feel that they too are experiencing the fulfillment of which Trist speaks, they will become disenchanted with teaching. About five years ago, I collaborated with Tom Walker (now at Temple University) on a small project that illustrates the contrast between dysfunctional and functional learning communities. Our goal was to enhance the self-esteem of high school students in vocational-education programs. We dreamed up the idea of having the high school students plan a demonstration of something they did or created in the auto shop, the carpentry shop, the beauty shop, the food-preparation shop, the store, or the hospital room that would be of interest to kindergarten children. All of the teachers save one agreed to participate. When we entered the holdout teacher's room, he came rushing out from behind his office/overseer's desk and started to berate the students. He told us that none of them had scored above the eightieth percentile on a basic math test. "Let me ask you something," he said, his face contorted with frustration; "could you take a rusty old car and make it into a shiny new one?" I could see where he was leading, so I said, "That depends." He went on: "These kids don't even know how to add and subtract! How can they expect me to teach them carpentry? They just make stupid mistakes and waste what little material we have." "They seem like a capable group of students to me," I said and walked away to admire the students' work, leaving the sputtering teacher to my more diplomatic colleague.

In the carpentry shop next door, the mood was radically different. In that class, a kind, supportive teacher was asking questions, making suggestions, and chuckling together with students about the mistakes that had been averted. This group of high school students showed the children how to build a simple piece of climbing equipment, then donated the item to the five-year-olds for classroom use. The kindergarteners were impressed that anyone could create such a substantial toy, and they heaped adulation on their "big kid" friends. The high school students visited the kindergarten and had the opportunity to see them playing delightedly with the finished project. A functional learning community is more like a family, which is what we should be striving to become (Hillman, 1988).

A Learning Community in Action

As I pull into the driveway, the first thing I notice is that the grounds are lovely, accented by bright flowers of pink or purple rhododendron and masses of spring bulbs. I later learn that the flowerbeds are planned and maintained by student volunteers. The principal is enthusiastic yet reserved as he shows me around. We stop in several classrooms. I can best describe the atmosphere of these classes as "workshops," in the most positive sense. Children are intensely involved in various learning projects, they are consulting with peers and the teacher, they are so absorbed that they barely notice visitors. There is structure here, but it seems to facilitate rather than oppress. By most people's standards, many of these children would be categorized as "at risk," part of the rural poor. A tow-headed boy who has just completed a brass etching in art class holds it up with glee, and the principal catches his eye. They exchange smiles, and the child comes over to talk animatedly about his work. As we walk down the hall, I ask about the grade level, and the principal tells me that they are mixed-age groups, something that "seemed like a scheduling nightmare at first, but actually made things more efficient."

I have lunch with the teachers. Their animated conversation includes some real professional sharing. An English teacher calls out to a colleague: "Suzy! I loved the children's books about mammals. I'm glad there are science teachers who know about the process approach to writing!" Rose, a silver-haired math teacher, has been doing a "medieval marketplace" experience with the children as part of a unit on economics. This year, at the urging of her colleagues, she submitted it as a curriculum idea to a teachers' magazine, and it was published. A sign on the bulletin board reads: "Do we have good ideas, or what?" In a pocket below are copies of Rose's one-page description of the project. Several teachers grab one for later reading; Rose volunteers to help anyone else who wants to get an idea published. A child stops by the lounge and is ushered in; she just forgot to give the teacher her early-dismissal note. The teachers accept the interruption with equanimity. Evidently, this teachers' lounge has none of the inner-sanctum mystique. One of the teachers asks about her rap-group T-shirt, and the child leaves, looking rather satisfied that none of the teachers has even heard of the group. The librarian comes in to finalize the schedule for the upcoming visit of a children's author. The visit is being supported through a small grant from the district office. Finally, the conversation rolls around to the presentation I am about to give. Not all of the teachers are attending; only the teachers, parents, and administrators who have expressed an interest in "whole language" are participating. This scenario illustrates the essential features of a school learning community.

Characteristics of Learning Communities

To institute an open system, a learning community, people must do at least five things (Combs & Avila, 1985; Dodd & Rosenbaum, 1986; Eisner, 1988; Rogers, 1985).

1. *They must develop mutual trust and respect among all members.* Every profession includes some people who will be threatened by change. Quite predictably, inadequate teachers will feel exposed and vulnerable.

> The collegial setting is least satisfying to the least-prepared whose shaky hold in subject matter and uninspired teaching is unmasked in the collegial environment. This is necessary but

sad, and it takes a long time to remedy, for the least competent teachers learn both subject matter and teaching practices more slowly than do the others. It is natural that they would want to hide in their classrooms. Nevertheless, the charisma of the most inspired teachers should dominate the environment. Where it does, the learning climate can change quite rapidly—far more so than conventional wisdom would predict (Joyce, Murphy, Showers & Murphy, 1989, p. 77).

Even though it may be difficult to respect the least competent individuals for their teaching, we can respect them as human beings and support any signs of vitality or improvement in their teaching.

But marginal teachers are not the only ones who may resist a community structure. Those individuals who have learned to work the system to their advantage, who enjoy some privileged status founded on individual achievement, may be reluctant to abandon their successful coping strategies as well. For them, the groups will have to meet their needs for belonging, esteem, and power, or they will go their separate ways.

2. *They must have opportunities to deal with ideas and values.* If most teachers were asked to describe their faculty meetings, they would describe a list of announcements and discussions about policies and procedures. It is seldom that any real instructional issues are brought up. To establish a learning community, small, task-oriented groups must come together to deal with substantive issues. These groups should establish direction, priorities, and values. The people within these groups must accept two important precepts: first, that they will deal with the logic of the argument rather than the personalities of those involved; and second, that conflict is inevitable, so there will be times when it is best to "agree to disagree."

3. *They must take responsibility for their own actions.* Colleagueship has been described as being responsible for ourselves but committed to one another. Assuming responsibility for our own actions rather than blaming others is an important step toward growth. When people speak of "learning from mistakes," the assumption is that they have made a humiliating blunder and learned never to repeat it again. But learning from mistakes is something very different from simply correcting errors. It means that we are *using* the mistake, studying it, almost relishing it as an opportunity for learning. Members of classroom learning communities recognize that:

Experimentation, risk-taking, flexibility, autonomy — all desirable attributes in a technological era — are antithetical to the traditional classroom and to traditional instruction. Changes are necessary if children are to acquire a mode of learning that places responsibility on them and that allows them the freedom to try, to test, to innovate and to be creative (Tetenbaum & Mulkeen, 1986, p. 99).

4. *They must freely explore possible alternatives, trying to be creative and innovative.* Being skeptical of change for change's sake, yet willing to try something new, is a difficult line to tread while so many bandwagons whiz by. But if we keep in mind what the words "creativity" and "innovation" really mean, then it is easy to see why learning communities are better environments for innovations and creations. "Innovate" literally means "to make new," while "creativity" is generally defined as the ability to make a novel idea or product from the recombination or juxtaposition of existing elements. Put simply, nothing is completely new. Even cutting-edge technology is a combination and refinement of what already exists in our world. Learning communities allow for risk-taking, which leads to new and exciting ideas.

5. *They must learn through interaction with colleagues.* A visitor from Japan who had lived in this country for six months asked her American host this question: "Why, in America, do you allow co-workers to make fools of themselves?" The host was taken aback, yet really could not refute the observation. She fumbled for an answer, then said: "I suppose it is because workers are often penalized for mistakes and they feel that if someone else is in error, it's none of their business. They may even feel that, at least for the moment, it raises their status in the eyes of authority." This view that co-workers have responsibility for one another is fundamental to a fully functioning learning community.

It is usually easier to think ourselves out of educational dilemmas if we draw upon several people's experiences and ideas rather than one person's. Three types of thinking are necessary if one is to become a top-notch practitioner: critical, practical, and artistic (Gage & Berliner, 1989). Some examples of critical thinking are taking everything into account, thinking about various interpretations, and considering possible contradictions; examples of practical thinking include considering cost-effectiveness or effects on the learner; and examples of artistic thinking are such things as going beyond the known data or acting intuitively (Gage & Berliner, 1989). Working together helps to shore up any real or perceived deficiencies and ultimately arrive at better solutions.

I attended a series of mandatory Madeline Hunter workshops in a school district several years ago at which the emphasis was on the individual. Each day, a teacher's name was drawn from a hat; at the next session, that person had to present a fifteen-minute lesson which put all of Hunter's principles into practice. But what actually happened, despite the staff developer's best efforts, was that the competent teachers were competent anyway and the incompetent ones were exposed. I can still remember the junior high school teacher who gave a mystifying explanation of weather systems with a yellowed map, obviously one of his few visual aids. After he had finished, his district-wide colleagues were supposed to say how they felt as learners. They were gentle, but there were unmistakable undercurrents of confusion and frustration. The teacher's wounded looks suggested that this "professional development" activity had only served to convince him that he was incapable of quality work and that he was the object of ridicule among his colleagues. Worse yet, I could not help wondering if some unsuspecting group of junior high school students would get the fallout from his degrading experience. When he needed personal and individual support, all he got was a public failure.

Learning Communities for Children

We know that learning together does a better job of satisfying needs for power and belonging than does working alone (Glasser, 1990). Goodlad's (1984) study *A Place Called School* found that opportunities for peer interaction are regarded by adolescents as the major reason for being in school. Rather than fighting this need for affiliation, educators need to harness its energy to promote learning. Here is what Lori, a sixth-grader, had to say about the use of book-discussion groups in her class:

> I think working with a group of people helps you to get along with people, and you can get a lot of ideas out of listening to the other people. When talking to other people in a group, you feel like you *can* say things, and you can talk. When you're with yourself, you can't get new ideas from other people. Being in groups changed my learning, because I can learn from the other people (p. 33).

A classroom learning community such as the one that Lori describes shares the following characteristics:

1. Students come to know each other.
2. Students learn to value what each has to offer.
3. The focus is on problem-solving and inquiry.
4. Students and teachers share responsibility and control.
5. Children learn through action, reflection, and demonstration.
6. Teachers establish a learning atmosphere that is predictable yet full of real choices (Short, 1990).

Administrators in Learning Communities

A principal once described his job as that of a "procurer-facilitator. I know or figure out what teachers need to do their jobs effectively, and I go about getting it for them or helping them to discover it within themselves." Skillful leaders in learning communities do not need the ego satisfaction of "school rule." Rather, they approach working with teachers as teachers approach children's writing, knowing when to stay out of it and let them work it out for themselves, knowing what to say or do to help them get "unstuck." Many times, just listening and being there is enough. In fact, the inquiry-group leaders in school learning communities are more often the instructional experts—the teachers—and less often the principals or other supervisory personnel.

There is one simple test of leadership for the learning community, a distinction originally framed by John Dewey: Is the focus of the group control or is the focus inquiry? Effective groups keep questioning, asking not only "How?" and "Why?" but also "Why not?" Leadership in the learning community requires displaying enthusiasm, giving positive feedback, exercising diplomacy, lending support, and interacting with teachers as trusted colleagues rather than as underlings.

If I had to describe the most positive classroom learning environments I have ever experienced as a learner or as a teacher, I would characterize the participants as having had an almost conspiratorial approach, a sort of "We're in this thing together, and it is unquestionably a worthy cause; let's plot our successful mission." True, the word conspiracy has a negative connotation, but I am referring to positive aspects such as an underground resistance effort against an oppressive government. The great leaders in education seem to be able to intensify this singularity of purpose and feeling of excitement to emerge as the natural leaders among a band of freedom-fighters.

Parents in Learning Communities

In the earliest days of our country, parents were as involved in education as they could possibly be. Community members often banded together to sponsor bringing a teacher to their community, and teachers frequently lived for a period of time with each of the families of the children whom they taught. There is little in the parent-involvement literature over the last half-century that does not talk about parents as partners in the educational enterprise or underscore the important role of parents as children's "first teachers." But, as Kagan (1989) contends, it may be time to redefine school relations with parents, given the sweeping changes in American families. Today's "typical" family is a single working mother with a child or children. Rather than expect her to volunteer and support the school, we should recognize that she probably needs support and a variety of services herself. This does not mean that we should abandon the old-fashioned conferences or parent-involvement programs, only to say that we should not use the yardstick of nostalgia with which to measure contemporary families. Nor does providing services to families mean that schools have to create and administer services for children. Rather, school personnel need to be aware of whatever resources are available in their communities and, to borrow Howard Gardner's term, to function as "brokers" for these services. The school may provide a meeting room or other facility for some services, but it should not allow its purpose to become diverted from learning, nor should it buckle under the weight of trying to be all things to all people.

Parents in a learning community are: well informed about their child's learning, invited to participate in a wide range of activities (but not judged harshly if they cannot), treated as collaborators and respected for their commitment to the child, which is necessarily different from that of the school.

Sustaining Learning Communities

Establishing and maintaining learning communities begins with the adults. The following principles of the teaching–learning process from Malcolm Knowles (1975) should guide our efforts:

Principle One: The process is dynamic, interactive, and cooperative.

Principle Two: The people in the process are more important than the information to be learned or the techniques to be used.

Principle Three: Each person participating in the program has responsibility for its success or failure.

Principle Four: The procedures to follow must be determined by the goals set by the learners.

Principle Five: Significant learning takes place when the goals have cognitive, affective, and motoric components.

Principle Six: Interpersonal relationships between the learner and the teacher must progress from a supportive climate to new and direct challenges.

Principle Seven: Evaluation should be a continuous process in the learning situation.

Principle Eight: Significant learning takes place in an appropriate climate of interpersonal relationships between and among learners.

The learning communities that adults create to foster children's learning must reflect our *telos* of learning. As McKenzie (1990) observes:

We must maintain and strengthen basic skills, but we should view those skills as the foundation on which to erect a towering cathedral . . . We know that it may take decades—even generations—before the spires are complete, but, like the master builders of long ago, we can imagine the shape of the future. The work of school people is a craft of the highest order, the craft of inventing the good (p. 156).

PART TWO

Teacher Learning and Professional Development

Chapter 4

TEACHERS AS LEARNERS

When a practitioner becomes a researcher into his own practice, he engages in a continuous process of self-education. When practice is repetitive administration of techniques to the same kinds of problems, the practitioner may look to leisure as a source of relief, or to early retirement; but when he functions as a researcher-in-practice, the practice itself is a source of renewal. The recognition of error, with its resulting uncertainty, can become a source of discovery rather than an occasion for self-defense.

—Donald A. Schon, 1983

IN the entire excellence-in-education movement, there has been little mention of ever making mistakes. In fact, the mistakes of teachers are supposed to be, if anything, stamped out. In the wake of all that criticism, we have practically forgotten that good teachers do learn from their mistakes and that the expert teacher's learning is a lifelong project.

The Learning Projects of Adults

A learning project can be any type of endeavor; a physical skill (such as learning to play golf), a creative outlet (such as cake decorating), a formal educational experience (such as pursuing a master's degree), and so forth. Using these criteria, think about one learning project you have undertaken recently. What was it? Why were you motivated to pursue the project? Who planned the project? Who evaluated it? What benefits did you derive from it?

Adult learners sometimes think that their practice of pursuing an interest intensively for a period of time is unusual, but actually it is quite common. As one teacher put it: "I seem to get on these 'kicks.' Last year, it was crafts projects. I dried flowers and plants, made them into wreaths, and sold them at the crafts show. This year, I'm taking a calligraphy class. Next year, I'm sure I'll be on a 'baby kick' because we are expecting our first child." As adults, our learning is anything but predictable, piecemeal, and plodding. We often learn by just "running across something," we tend to organize our learning in "chunks," and we frequently pursue an interest with great intensity for a time, then move on. One learning project that is large enough and sufficiently complex to hold our interest for an extended period of time is our work as professionals, the complex and demanding task of becoming "someone who engages learners, who seeks to involve each person wholly — mind, sense of self, sense of humor, range of interest, interactions with other people — in learning" (Duckworth, 1986, p. 490).

Important Features of Teachers' Learning

James Britton (1988) once said that "the word for teaching is learning," and there is now considerable research evidence to support his point of view. The following discussion expands on Britton's insight.

1. *The best teachers are active learners.* Arends (1983) studied the learning activities (primarily workshops, conferences, and university studies) of 34 beginning teachers. The average number of hours devoted to learning activities during the first three years was 623 for "avid" beginners, 295 for "average" beginners, and 32 for "reluctant" beginners. Administrators' ratings of the beginning teachers' effectiveness were clearly related to learning activities, leading the researcher to conclude that "the most competent teachers are the most avid learners" (Arends, 1983, p. 235).

> It has long been recognized that children learn more from adults' deeds than from their words. In order to develop a love of learning in students, teachers must first be learners themselves. Children do not become avid readers, for instance, through admonishment. They are motivated to read by others who have a contagious enthusiasm for literature. The same teachers who deplore children's reading achievement typically do not themselves peruse professional publications, take pleasure in the latest bestseller, or even become familiar with the books that are read by their students. There is no satisfactory substitute for teaching scholarship through example (Jalongo, 1986, pp. 355, 356).

2. *Teaching knowledge must be constructed.* Carl Rogers (1969) once said, "It seems to me that anything that can be taught to another is relatively inconsequential. I have come to feel that the only learning which significantly influences behavior is self-

discovered, self-appropriated learning." Unfortunately, Rogers's statement has sometimes been as misinterpreted as John Dewey's call for progressive education. Neither of these great educators was recommending an abdication of professional responsibility. They were advocating that teachers function as facilitators of learning rather than as founts of information that deluge children with droplets of information, hoping that some will sink in. Just as children need to build their own understandings, teachers need the guidance and support of fellow professionals to build their under-standings of what it means to teach. Reeves and Kazelskis (1985) explain personal construct systems this way:

> Knowledge of reality is constructed by each person, is active and continually open to reinterpretation of meaning, is not an aggregation of learned "fact," and is not restricted to "informa-tion input" received by the person (p. 271).

At its simplest, this means that we learn by successive approxima-tions. Each teacher gradually builds a theory of the world of teach-ing and continually tests this theory in the classroom. We envision a classroom scenario or play out a script before teaching and then stick with that scenario or script unless something goes wrong during the lesson (Parker, 1984). And what is the thing that is most likely to "go wrong," signaling to a teacher that a change in behavior is necessary? Usually, it is the perception of a lack of student interest (Parker, 1984). Preservice or inservice educators may be given information, but it is up to them to integrate and use that information. No one can simply tell them how to teach.

3. *Teachers' learning experiences need to meet their individual needs.* When we hear teachers talk about the learning experiences planned for them by others, the fact that nouns are so frequently changed into verbs is very telling. Teachers talk about being "inserviced," about being "mentored" or "developed professionally" —all grammatical constructions which suggest that they are more passive than active. In a nationwide study of inservice teachers conducted by Stanford University, the researchers concluded that teachers perceive opportunities for furthering their education as "weak, improverished and a relative failure" (Joyce, Howey & Yarger, 1976, p. xvii). An understanding of adult development suggests why. Adults need learning experiences which are indi-vidualized and practical, that require active participation in functional tasks.

Teachers' needs for professional development vary considerably, depending upon such things as their interests and skills, their teaching assignments, and their experiential backgrounds (McLaughlin, Pfeifer, Swanson-Owens & Yee, 1986). Teachers are bound to be dissatisfied if a visiting expert gives them a lecture outside their range of interest, incommensurate with their skills, unrelated to their assignment, or unconnected to their experience. Take, for example, a presentation on children's study skills. Some teachers may feel little responsibility for or interest in developing children's study skills. Others may be interested but fail to see how the particular program presented would apply to their specific situation. For still others, the session may be both interesting and applicable but not pitched at their level of skill—either too basic or too complex. If any of these things occur, you can overhear them in the hallway afterward, explaining that they would rather be working in their classrooms than sitting in meetings all day.

Paradoxically, teachers' learning is both highly individual and highly collaborative:

> Teachers need the freedom to develop their own unique styles. They need to develop repertoires and learn to vary their approaches according to the situation. Improvement of instruction implies change and change in teaching behavior requires professional and intellectual stimulation as well as social support (Hoy & Woolfolk, 1989, p. 129).

4. *Teachers' learning is not restricted to formal classroom experiences.* Teachers are extending their learning further all the time. If we looked at the ability level of teachers in Colonial times or the skills of a schoolmarm in the American West, we would be appalled. Most of these teachers were barely literate themselves, but their skills were considerably more sophisticated than those of the average person and were therefore valued. Today, more than half of the teachers in America hold master's degrees, and five percent hold doctorates (Joyce, Howey & Yager, 1976). Where teachers' learning is concerned, these formal learning experiences are a small part of what they actually learn. Teachers also participate in workshops and conferences, visit exemplary programs, log inservice credits, and read and discuss professional writings.

5. *Teachers who are enthusiastic learners have greater insight into children's learning.* When teachers are frequently cast in the role of learner, they have greater sensitivity to the needs of learners

in their classroom. They quickly ascertain, as Theodore Roethke once observed, that it is the cardinal sin of an educator to be boring.

Imagine that an announcement of an all-day Saturday workshop for teachers is posted on the bulletin board. What will determine whether or not you sign up? If you are like most of us, your decision will be affected by the answers to these questions:

Does it sound interesting? Could it be boring?

How relevant is the topic? How much value will it have for my teaching?

What is the reputation of the person conducting the workshop?

Can I get support from my district to attend?

Can I stand to give up a Saturday and be in class all day?

Note that the first three considerations usually determine whether you will pursue the last two logistical questions.

Being on the receiving end of teaching, both good or poor, can be deeply affecting. If the workshop is wonderful, we are anxious to try out what we have learned; if the workshop is terrible, we are more mindful of how deadly dull classroom activities can be.

6. *Teachers who are active learners become researchers into their own practice.* When teachers examine their own practice, inquiry becomes the focal point. They are curious about what their students think and pose questions to children. They also ask themselves questions such as these, suggested by Eleanor Duckworth (1986, p. 490):

How do people think about these matters?

Which ideas build on which others and how? Which interests build on other interests?

Which ideas get in the way of other ideas?

How does an idea get modified?

How does a firmly held conviction influence how a person reads an experience?

What is the range of conceptions covered by a "right-sounding" work or phrase?

In what circumstances is a person confused by / deaf to / helped by another person's thoughts?

What factors keep interest high?

How does a specific representation of one's thoughts influence how the thoughts develop further?

How does an idea lead to a new question, and *vice-versa?*

7. *Teachers who are avid learners themselves have high expectations for students.* When a teacher is fully committed to learning, she or he has a sense of efficacy. Efficacy is the teacher's belief that

he or she can help even the most difficult or unmotivated students (McLaughlin & Marsh, 1978). Efficacy beliefs are a key to teachers' professional growth, children's learning, and child advocacy (Fennimore, 1989). Even though a teacher's faith is sometimes shaken, the truth is that there is no compelling and personally satisfying reason to get up in the morning and go to school without those efficacy beliefs. Teachers' professional development and children's learning are rooted in the teacher's experience as a learner, just as having been a child in a family influences our behavior within the families we later create as adults.

Adult Learning Theory

In all of the recent reform proposals for teacher education that I have examined, one important source of information and direction has been virtually ignored: adult learning theory. Adult learning theory, or andragogy, is the art and science of helping adults learn. Actually, andragogy is a relatively recent development. Until the 1970s, the prevailing attitude was that, in contrast to the rapid changes of childhood or the tumult of adolescence, adulthood remains essentially the same from the age of 21 to dotage. Now that people are living longer and the majority rule in America is the over-forty crowd, adult development is coming into its own. Bestselling books such as Gail Sheehy's *Passages,* which draws heavily upon the research of Roger Gould, speak to a burgeoning interest in adult development.

The key to understanding adult development is to recognize that, under anything approximating normal conditions, human beings will tend to seek growth. Just think of all the expressions we use that reflect this orientation. People who abandon a career speak of "getting nowhere," of "being in a dead-end job," of feeling that they are "losing ground" or have suffered a "setback." Five basic assumptions about how adults learn and grow (Knowles, 1975) apply to teachers:

1. Teachers' self-concepts move from dependency to self-direction.

2. Teachers learn primarily by tapping into their experiences and reflecting upon them.

3. Teachers are motivated to learn by their desire to fulfill social roles.

4. Teachers are interested in learning today what helps them teach better tomorrow (immediacy of application).

5. Teachers want information which helps them solve specific

problems rather than information for its own sake (problem-centeredness rather than subject-centeredness).

Adult Motivation to Learn

In addition to the what and how of adult learning, there is also the why. From a sociological and psychological perspective, there are three basic motivators and ways of valuing work: money, autonomy, and recognition. More specifically, adults are categorically motivated to seek growth by any one or all of the following:

• *Desire to achieve practical goals,* to get a new job, advance in a current one, or increase income

• *Desire to achieve personal satisfaction and other inner-directed goals,* such as personal development and family well-being

• *Desire to gain new knowledge,* including the desire to learn for its own sake

• *Desire to achieve formal education goals,* such as degrees or certification

• *Desire to socialize with others,* and escape from everyday routine

• *Desire to achieve societal goals,* to exert an influence on the community (Cross, 1981)

Every teacher has the choice of seeking growth or resisting growth as a learner. If the choice is made to stop learning, then children's learning will atrophy as well, and the major satisfaction of teaching will be gone. But if teachers make a conscious decision to pursue learning throughout their lives and share their discoveries and enthusiasms with their students, then children's learning will be facilitated. Ultimately, as the philosopher Jean-Paul Sartre concluded, "We *are* our choices."

Chapter 5

STAGES IN
TEACHERS' PROFESSIONAL DEVELOPMENT

If you treat an individual as he is, he will stay as he is, but if you treat him as if he were what he ought to be and could be, he will become what he ought to be and what he could be.

—Goethe

WHENEVER I talk to a group of teachers about the general sequence for teachers' development, they usually seem rather surprised. Surprised, I think, that anyone would care enough to study them and bemused by how accurately these themes and stages characterize their own professional experience.

Themes in Teacher Development

One of the most helpful ways of conceptualizing major themes in teacher development originated with Frances Fuller (Fuller, 1969; Fuller & Bown, 1975). She concluded that, generally speaking, teachers' dominant concerns moved from a focus on *self* to a focus on *task* and, finally, to a focus on *impact*.

Focus on self. New teachers are usually preoccupied with their own ability to function in the teaching role. When they look back on that first year, it is often with some regret for their students. "How much damage did my foolish mistakes do?" they often wonder. Despite teacher preparation experiences to the contrary, beginning teachers frequently feel insecure and regress to more familiar types of teacher behavior. Ironically, that behavior is often the most pedestrian teaching that they experienced themselves as children. Some common concerns of beginning teachers are that the students will misbehave, be bored, dislike them, or ask questions that they cannot answer.

The challenge to novice teachers is to move beyond exploration, fantasy, and fears about the teaching role. They must reconstruct their concept of teacher in a personal, nonstereotypical, and confident way.

Focus on task. Gradually, teachers move from a focus on themselves to a focus on the task. "How am I doing?" and "How can I do it better?" seem to be the dominant concerns. As concerns about their ability to perform in the role of teacher diminish, teachers focus on the task. A teacher in her third year expressed these task-focused worries: "I am concerned about not having the resources to accomplish what I want to do. I also worry about not being supported by administrators and peers. It is sometimes difficult to involve parents in their children's education. I worry that, without their support, I won't be able to help children enough."

Focus on impact. The move to master teacher demands more. It is no longer sufficient to do what is expected. Now teachers ask themselves: "Will what I have taught make a difference, not just for this week, the end of the unit, or even the academic year? Will it have some enduring significance?" Maturing teachers are people who have

> taken some steps toward making explicit their theories and beliefs about learners, curriculum, subject matter and the teacher's role. This teacher has developed a style of planning for instruction that includes several interrelated types of planning and that has become more streamlined and automatic with experience. Much of this teacher's interactive teaching consists of routines familiar to the students, thus decreasing the collective information processing load. During teaching, the teacher attends to and intently processes academic and nonacademic sociocognitive events and cues. These experienced teachers have developed the confidence to depart from a planned course of action when they judge that to be appropriate. They reflect on and analyze the apparent effects of their own teaching and apply the results of these reflections to their future plans and actions (Clark & Peterson, 1986, pp. 292–93).

In addition to these dominant themes in teacher development, theory and research have identified specific stages.

Stages in Teacher Development
Many different authors have described the sequence of teachers' professional development in considerable detail (Heath, 1986;

Ryan, 1986; Swick & Hanes, 1987). Understanding this progression can inform teachers about their own developmental milestones and better equip them to function as colleagues with teachers at various stages.

Preservice teachers. Preservice teachers are still in the process of making their career decision about teaching. They usually have the idealism characteristic of their age, but they are also fearful of failure. Here is how one college sophomore described her "teaching nightmare": "I will be so nervous that I can hardly speak. The kids will look at me as if I have two heads and be distracted by *anything* in the room. My activities will be finished in half the time I thought, and the kids are practically sleeping through my lesson. When someone finally does ask a question, I don't know the answer. I leave feeling as if they would be better off if I had not even been there."

The student teaching experience. Near the end of a semester of student teaching, Delfina writes the following entry in her student-teaching journal:

"I had no idea that teaching was so hard. I mean, it looks easy when you are sitting at your desk watching a terrific teacher in action. I thought it was tough when I had to prepare and teach a handful of lessons in my methods courses. Now I have all subjects every day during my last two weeks of student teaching. It is going well, but it takes *so much* to make it go well. What is that slogan— 'The toughest job you'll ever love'? I love it, but I go home every day exhausted, not so much physically but mentally and emotionally. By Friday, I go home and go directly to sleep!"

The classroom teacher and university supervisor who are working with Delfina empathize, but they also try to prepare her for the shock of that first year. They do this because:

> Student teaching is a reality test, but it is a sheltered reality... the hard work of establishing a classroom culture already has been done; and whether student teachers know it or not, they are simply maintaining the system already established. While this is no mean feat, the student teacher is simply not the teacher (Ryan, 1986, p. 12).

First year / survival. The situation of new teachers is not that of "a stranger in a strange land" but a role reversal in a familiar setting: they have amassed many hours in schools as students but comparatively few in the professional role of teacher.

The average teacher has had, including higher education, about 60 teachers from whom admirable behaviors, skills and attitudes can be selected and imitated. As a result of all this exposure to models, teachers have a large storehouse of images of school life (Ryan, 1986, p. 17).

In spite of the extensive vicarious experience, new teachers are shocked by several things: the stamina required of the job, the amount of paperwork, the range and intensity of students' needs, the parents who lack confidence in them, and the lack of support for their efforts within the school and district (Ryan, 1986).

Ms. Gilbert was one teacher who experienced such a shock. She had been such an outstanding student teacher that she earned an award. In August, she was hired to work in a large inner-city high school. She happened to run into her university supervisor and confided: "It isn't what I expected at all. The things that I was rewarded for as a student teacher seem to be a source of annoyance to these teachers. One even said to me, 'Why are you working so hard? You're making the rest of us look bad.' Another talked with me about my science unit and, just when I thought he was genuinely interested in the project, he said, 'Well, just remember—we don't have merit pay yet.' Even though they criticize me for working hard, I am constantly 'volunteered' to take on all sorts of additional responsibilities at school because, according to the other teachers, I am young and single, so I have the time and energy. The supervisor just sticks her head in the door and asks how it's going. My principal seems impressed and gave me an excellent evaluation, but she—these are her words—has 'learned to survive by avoiding controversy.' Maybe I was unrealistic about what teaching is like. It would probably be easier for everyone, including myself, to conform and lower my standards."

Nearly every teacher has experienced some sort of negative socialization—a time when a few "misery loves company" teachers tried to talk him or her into doing less and doing it poorly to help themselves feel less threatened. One master teacher who read Ms. Gilbert's story put it this way: "Twenty years ago, I was Ms. Gilbert." If you interviewed her about her teacher-preparation program, Ms. Gilbert would be generally positive yet feel that the university had failed to prepare her for the realities of teaching.

The Myth of Thorough Preparation

"I never cared less whether I lived or died than I did during my first year of teaching." This is how Garrett Keizer (1988) begins his book about becoming a high school teacher. Whenever I share that line with teachers, I see knowing looks and rueful smiles. No matter how well they were prepared, the responsibility for the learning of a diverse group of human beings, the need to make hundreds of decisions every day, the pressure to know what to do, and the courage to do what is right can be simply overwhelming to novice teachers. Colleges of education have been roundly criticized for failing to do a better job. There are several reasons why teacher-preparation programs cannot fully prepare teachers for what they will encounter in a classroom.

1. *Change versus status quo.* In every teacher-preparation program, there is a conflict between preparing educators to become change agents and preparing teachers for schools as they are today. If undergraduate teacher preparation reflects the most up-to-date information as it should, that theory and research may not have filtered into some classrooms yet, and new teachers may feel "out of sync" with their new colleagues.

2. *General versus specific.* Teacher preparation has to prepare teachers for a wide range of possibilities. In many states, elementary teachers are certified to teach kindergarten through sixth grade while secondary teachers are certified junior high through twelfth grade. But when a newly certified teacher gets a specific teaching assignment—such as teaching fourth-grade social studies in a departmentalized elementary school—much of that general preparation seems irrelevant.

3. *Real versus ideal.* In the years before early field experience, when a prospective teacher's only face-to-face teaching was confined to a single semester, there were many horror stories about this "sink or swim" approach. Preparing teachers in this way was comparable to practicing swimming motions on dry land for three and a half years and then tossing students into the ocean. Even though introductions to the "real world" of teaching now occur more often and earlier, colleges of education cannot eradicate those feelings of inadequacy during the first year. Teacher-preparation programs try to build the beginning teacher's skills and confidence. If idealistic prospective teachers were presented with all of the realities of the classroom at the onset of their preparation, it would probably create a major teacher shortage. Students are taught to drive, but not on icy roads with bald tires.

4. *Promise versus perfection.* Teacher educators are in the business of making predictions about who will become effective classroom teachers. We observe students in the context of the college classroom and make inferences about how they will function as preservice teachers. Then we observe them in someone else's classroom with someone else's students and render professional judgments about how they will function as inservice teachers. We do not expect them to be perfect in either situation; we are looking for promise and growth. Sometimes, we are wrong to give second chances, sometimes we are right. I am reminded of a student who failed my class and then, due to a colleague's retirement, ended up in my section of the same course again. I withheld judgment the second time around, and this young woman proved to be a terrific teacher. When I asked her what had happened the first time, she simply said, "Too much sorority." On graduation day, I met her entire family. Her mother looked at me curiously, evidently wondering about a professor who could give the same student an "F" one semester and an "A" the next. We chatted about the student's remarkable transformation, and her mother commented on the letter of recommendation I had written. "Brenda read it to me over the telephone long distance — twice. We're so proud of her. She's the first one in our family to ever go to college and today she's *graduating.*"

These three issues — (1) the fact that preservice teacher education must develop student potential and predict eventual success, (2) the need to keep prospective teachers' idealism alive, and (3) the emphasis on change rather than preserving the *status quo* — help to illustrate why a good teacher-preparation program can inaugurate the teacher's journey as a learner but never fully prepare him or her to teach. Each teacher must make the difficult adjustment from the academic world to the real world of the classroom (Moffett, St. John & Isken, 1987). Even when teachers are equipped with a repertoire of effective teaching behaviors, they still have to decide which to use, when and how to use them, and which students to use them with (Clark & Yinger, 1977). Much of the craft of teaching must be learned on the job (Ryan, 1986).

Experienced Teachers

After most teachers have survived their first two or three years, their role is more clearly defined and they begin to focus on the consolidation and refinement of their teaching strategies. If they are to become expert teachers, this stage is characterized by experimentation and an expansion of the teaching repertoire rather than desperate attachment to whatever enabled them to survive. Often, they begin to question generally accepted practice, as did this kindergarten teacher:

> My concern is that as more and more companies publish kindergarten workbooks, worksheets, ditto materials, letters to parents and that sort of thing, I see a huge volume of printed material for kindergarten becoming available and I'm not always sure that is the best way for children to learn. I find myself doing more and more ditto materials, more and more workbooks and this kind of thing when I really don't feel that they learn that much or learn that way (Freeman & Hatch, 1987, p. 22).

After good teachers have accumulated four or more years of experience, they usually begin to reappraise their situation and seek renewal. The theme of having a lasting impact on students tends to dominate. Often, their concerns are precipitated by critical incidents that cause them to re-evaluate their professional lives. Here is how one teacher described a critical incident that prompted her to seek renewal:

"Back in my undergraduate days, I thought that Dr. Jelliot was the best professor on campus. We felt that we were learning so much—all the particulars of phonics and grammar, all about basals and how to disguise practice and drill with cute little games to keep the children 'on task.' I taught that way for years and barely questioned it. Then I was sitting in the lounge grading some papers when Jeff, a colleague who teaches science, picked up one of my papers and looked at it. 'Geez, Helen, I don't think *I* could pass this test. What good is a "schwa" sound, anyway? A hundred years from now, will anyone care?' I was put on the defensive and covered up by joking about some piece of trivia from his field, but it got me thinking. Jeff's offhanded remark had hit a nerve. I was really starting to rethink everything about the way I teach. I started to wonder if the kids were learning in spite of me instead of because of me. During the summer, I went back to school. Dr. Jelliott had retired, and I studied with three new faculty members whose philosophies matched the one that was emerging in me. I came back to school that fall feeling revitalized."

In most conceptualizations of teachers' developmental stages, reappraisal and renewal such as this continue until teachers reach the conclusion of their classroom careers.

The final stage in teacher development is disengagement, a time when teachers prepare for retirement and review their lives in classrooms. In Erik Erikson's (1950) terms, the crisis to be resolved is "integrity versus despair." A life well spent builds integrity while the feeling of wasted human potential elicits feelings of frustration and despair. The experiences of two teachers exemplify these very different outcomes.

Several years ago, I was having dinner with a group of administrators before speaking at the PTA meeting that evening. One principal was discussing a teacher in his building who was past the official retirement age but was, in his words, "still going strong and still one of our finest teachers." As the conversation continued, I realized that he was talking about Miss Burkett, the fourth-grade teacher who had inspired my sister to become a teacher and had encouraged my mother to become a "room mother." I remembered the day that Miss Burkett visited our home, bearing a gift for my new baby sister. When we met, she gently lifted my shy seven-year-old face with her hand. I felt that she could see everything that was in my mind and heart—that even if what she saw were "Unsatisfactory," she would know what to do to make it "Outstanding." When admirable teachers such as Miss Burkett approach the end of their teaching careers, they have a sense of completion and satisfaction.

But what about the teacher whose life review uncovers dissatisfaction? One of the best examples of this negative outcome was described by one of my graduate students:

"Somehow, I got elected to plan a retirement party for one of the teachers. She is best known for her 'little red wagon,' which she pulls from the office to her classroom, loaded down with dittos. She is also known for being negative. Everything that is suggested, she has done it before and it didn't work. I think what really pushed her out the door was when our new principal said that he was shutting down the ditto machine until he saw the more literature-based curriculum we have been working on for several years. This woman went into a tizzy and decided it was time to 'hang up her wagon,' as one of the other teachers put it. Getting people to come to her retirement party was like pulling teeth, but I managed to get a respectable showing by begging and playing on their sympathies. Everyone was sitting there, making the best of the social obligation, when the guest of honor stood up to speak. We expected kind words, but what we got instead was hostility! She said that we were a bunch of hypocrites because we were all happy to see her leave, and on and on. Then she stormed out. Afterward, everyone was sarcastically thanking me for a lovely evening. It's a good thing she moved to Florida, because I think she would have been practically ostracized around here."

What caused feelings of such intense bitterness at the conclusion of this teacher's career? What steps could have been taken to avoid this frustration and despair? We can only speculate about the kinds and amount of various experiences that would have made her professional life review more positive. For many teachers, working successfully, not only with children but with other professionals, is another important way of seeking growth.

Experts and Novices: Mentor-Protégé Relationships

The concept of mentorship is an ancient one. The original Mentor was the tutor, role model, and confidant of Odysseus' son. Ever since that time, a mentor has been an extraordinary role model who validates, supports, and facilitates the professional growth of a novice. When people talk about mentoring, they usually emphasize the benefits to the newcomer (Gehrke & Ray, 1984). Actually, the interpersonal relationship is beneficial to the mentor as well. Many expert teachers derive great satisfaction from working with beginning teachers because they are helping to resolve the developmental issue of "generativity versus stagnation" (Erikson, 1950). At this stage, making a contribution to the development of novices can be particularly fulfilling (Fagan & Walter, 1983). Expert teachers who succeed as mentors experience growth because, "just as becoming a classroom teacher involves making a transition from person to professional, so too becoming a mentor involves making a transition from classroom teacher to teacher educator" (Feinman-Nemser & Buchmann, 1987, p. 272).

Problems with Mentoring in Education

In recent years, many schools have latched onto the idea of mentoring, which is widely practiced in business organizations and graduate education, and have instituted "mentor teacher" programs in basic education. Ideally, these program are designed to simultaneously support beginning teachers and give recognition to master teachers. But too many schools have compromised the concept of mentoring in the process (Jalongo, 1988). Joan's experience as a protégé illustrated four reasons why.

First of all, Joan was assigned to her mentor without ever having met her. In real mentoring, the relationship is voluntary, spontaneous, and built on reciprocal trust. Authentic mentor–protégé relationships cannot be forced. True, a small percentage of assigned matches will work out, but that is attributable to good luck and good people, not a testimonial to the success of the program. Second, most of these mentoring plans assume that all master teachers are mentor teachers. Mentoring programs that make this assumption are apt to get some responses such as this one from an elderly man who was commenting on intergenerational child-care programs: "Everybody thinks just because I'm an old man I'm supposed to like children. Well, I didn't like them when I was young and I don't like them any better now." The same sentiment can be applied to the relationship between master teachers and beginning teachers: the fact that master teachers are adept at working with children themselves does not mean that they are especially willing to share that expertise or know how to go about developing it in adults. The ability to become an effective mentor is not commonplace, and even those who possess the ability need preparation for this important role.

Furthermore, not everyone wants to do what is expected of mentor teachers. Some mentor teachers are obligated to accept eleven-month contracts, serve on many different committees, or spend most of their time with new teachers when they would prefer to devote full time to classroom teaching (Moore, 1984). Worse yet is the misconception that marginal teachers can be renewed by becoming mentors. It is a basic principle of human development that a person's own needs must be met before he or she can contribute to the development of others.

A fourth and final confusion of mentoring is mixing it with evaluation. Joan's mentor told her: "Remember that at the end of your first year, I have to be the one who evaluates you. If you are having problems, don't mention them to me because, if you do, I will be forced to make a note of it. It's better for you to find another confidant because I am responsible for writing a report on your progress at the end of the year." Mentorships will work in education only if they permit free and reciprocal choice of mentors and protégés, only if mentors are selected carefully and prepared for the role, and only if mentors are kept out of the business of formal evaluation.

Self-Esteem and Success in Teaching

Professional self-esteem is a combination of the four markers of success in our society:

1. Competence — the ability to perform adequately
2. Significance — gaining recognition and attention for efforts
3. Power — the ability to influence others
4. Virtue — engaging in ethical behavior (Coopersmith, 1981)

If a teacher knows that he or she is generally regarded as outstanding, it may be gratifying, but it may also be worrisome. Teachers may fear success because it establishes a mark which they feel obligated to hit or surpass all the time. They may also remain insecure and, despite ample evidence of their success, feel like imposters.

In a school which is intensely hierarchical and competitive, those who have been singled out as excellent feel even more vulnerable. A survey of California mentor teachers, for example, revealed that some teachers opted to keep their talent to themselves and abandon the project rather than risk the resentment of co-workers over what was perceived as preferential status (Ralston, 1990). This sort of sentiment has to change if schools are to realize their full human potential. We cannot fear excellence simply because every person is not excellent, nor can we abuse our finest teachers by expecting them to be uniformly excellent every minute of the day.

Learning communities will contribute to professional growth if we heed this advice from Thoreau: "Beware of all enterprises that require new clothes, and not rather a wearer of new clothes." Teachers have to become those new wearers or the changes made will be superficial and add to our already-cluttered educational "wardrobes" rather than contribute to the quality of our schools.

Chapter 6

ISSUES IN THE
PROFESSIONAL DEVELOPMENT OF TEACHERS

Self-development is a higher duty than self-sacrifice.
                              —Elizabeth Cady Stanton, 1848

RECENTLY, I spoke with a master teacher who had traveled to Australia. The study of Australia was part of her social-studies curriculum, and she was seeking both personal and professional development through travel. She had saved for years and took the journey "because, you know, in this job you have to take care of yourself." The idea that a teacher should be in charge of his or her own professional development may seem like a rather startling concept. Educators are, as a group, very altruistic; they would expect a great teacher's life to be a path of self-sacrifice rather than a plan for self-fulfillment. But becoming a master teacher is not a choice between attending to our professional growth and the needs of others; it is doing both. The belief that "dedicated" teachers deny their needs and attend exclusively to the needs of students is clearly outmoded and inaccurate. Becoming a teacher involves forging an individual identity within the professional role. The word "individual" here is important because it literally means indivisible. No matter how supportive of their teachers' professional growth institutions become, it is up to teachers to identify their needs for growth and plan an agenda for personal–professional fulfillment.

Taking Charge of Professional Development

Teachers who learn to take care of themselves professionally are not selfish; they are smart. As architects of their professional growth, they recognize how their level of satisfaction influences relationships with colleagues and ultimately affects children's learning.

The first assumption of professional development is that it is a complex, human task. It requires a climate conducive to learning and change . . . It is promoted by the effective use of diverse resources. It includes opportunities for field-testing, feedback, and adjustment. All of these things take time to achieve (Wood, Thompson & Russell, 1981, p. 88).

Despite the obvious importance of professional development, there are many reasons why teaching has been deprofessionalized.

The Concept of Professionalism

Too often, the word "professionalism" is used as a barb to put teachers in their place. Teachers supposedly exhibit a "lack of professionalism" when they challenge administrative policies or procedures, rally around a cause, or do almost anything that results in bad publicity. Actually, professionalism involves four things:

- A defined body of specialized knowledge not possessed by the general public
- Control over licensure, certification, entrance requirements, and standards for responsible practice
- Autonomy of practitioners to apply that knowledge in diverse situations, to make decisions, and to exercise judgment
- High prestige and economic standing in the larger community (Darling-Hammond, 1987; Ornstein, 1981; Weinstein, 1989)

It has been argued on the basis of these criteria that teaching is not a profession. Forests have been depleted by the papers produced in debating this semantic point. For the purposes of this discussion, let us simply begin to call teachers experts. This word, it seems to me, carries less excess baggage and frees us to focus on the positive side of things instead of making comparisons between teaching and medicine or law, comparisons in which education appears deficient. If anyone wants to argue that there is not a specialized expertise associated with teaching, I invite them to consider Donald Quinn's (1984) description of teaching:

If a doctor, or lawyer, or dentist had forty people in his office at one time, all of whom had different needs, and some of whom didn't want to be there and were causing trouble, and the doctor, lawyer, or dentist, without assistance had to treat them all with professional excellence for nine months, then he might have some conception of the classroom teacher's job (p. 81).

Uniqueness of the Teaching Profession

As a profession, teaching has many uniquenesses (Swick & Hanes, 1987). First of all, teachers are compulsory participants in state- and university-mandated acts. They must meet state certification requirements and perform a public service. Furthermore, unlike most other professionals, they usually have little or nothing to say about who their "clients" will be. Yet, under normal conditions, their work involves hundreds of hours in the company of these clients. Third, the test of a teacher's professional abilities is performance-oriented and situation-specific, determined by effectiveness in particular classrooms at particular times. Fourth, teacher education, while ostensibly focused on adults, is actually intended for children. Teachers have responsibility for their own learning *and* for the effects of that learning on children's learning. Finally, teaching is the only profession that virtually every person in America has had ample opportunity to observe, at least from the other side of the desk. The average high school graduate has spent more time in the company of teachers than in any pursuit other than sleeping or watching television (Ryan, 1986).

Sources of Professional Authority

Lee Shulman (1986, 1987) has identified seven areas of teacher expertise: (1) subject matter, (2) general pedagogy, (3) curriculum, (4) subject-specific teaching principles, (5) child development, (6) educational contexts, and (7) goals and values of education. To a considerable extent, professional stature in the larger community requires a body of expertise that is perceived as highly specialized by the general public. In teaching, this can prove rather difficult because practically everyone knows quite a bit about schools.

What is the most specialized knowledge of teachers? Some would say that it is pedagogy, teaching methods. But the layperson's familiarity with the methodology of teachers weakens its mystique. Some would say that it is content. But if that is a teacher's only unique body of knowledge, then early childhood teachers will be less respected than high school teachers because the content taught to adolescents is more abstract. Another difficulty with an emphasis on content is that the layperson is unlikely to be impressed by teaching-methods courses such as "Children's Literature" or "Teaching of Social Studies." If we want to impress the general public with the academic rigor of our teacher-preparation programs, teachers will have to take more difficult-sounding courses borrowed from other disciplines.

Actually, there is one body of knowledge that is directly applicable to the practitioner, academically rigorous, not widely understood by the layperson, and essential to autonomous decision-making (Moyer, 1986). That field is child development. Usually, child development is a single course taught early in the preservice teacher's career, encountered before the student has much experience to bring to its study. But, if you ask a group of experienced teachers where they would like to begin in improving their school curriculum, they are quick to perceive the need to further their understanding of child development. Their classroom experiences have convinced them of the value of, not just knowing what or even how, but also why. If we were to emphasize knowledge of child growth and development in our teacher-development programs, we would increase the social status of teachers, create more child-centered programs, build teachers' professional autonomy, and support teachers in their role as decision-makers.

Elements of Teacher Professionalism

The buzzwords which have dominated education over the past several decades reveal a common thread. Some of these words are: effectiveness ("Our teaching force is riddled with incompetence"), accountability ("Teachers need to be monitored closely"), burnout ("Our teachers are weary"), empowerment ("Our teachers need managers to pull them out of this slump"), and deprofessionalization ("Teachers deserve more respect"). The common thread among these words is another word — alienation. Human beings become alienated when their role is unclear, when their autonomy is threatened, and when they doubt their ability to work inside the organization to effect meaningful change (Seeman, 1959).

The antidote to alienation is for teachers to participate in more job-related discussions and to share their instructional decision-making processes and dilemmas with colleagues. As Fullan (1982) points out, it is the bond of shared understandings and common language that reduces feelings of stress and sustains innovations. To the degree that this professional interaction fails, the school is deprived of the collective wisdom of its faculty and teachers are deprived of opportunities for professional development (Feir, 1988). It would stand to reason, then, that if teachers are to end this alienation, they must achieve greater role clarity, function more autonomously, and focus on interactive decision-making processes.

Role Clarity

What is the best way to characterize the teaching role and teaching functions? For decades, there has been a nature/nurture controversy, a debate over whether good teachers are born or made. As a corollary to that issue, there is the art *vs.* craft *vs.* science argument. If we contend that good teachers are born, we have no power. If we argue that teaching is a craft or even a science, we deny the essentially human side of the teaching–learning dynamic.

In 1985, Eisner proposed that we think of the teacher as performing artist; many of the most forward-thinking trends in education are an outgrowth of this vision of teaching. Take, for example, the idea of teacher portfolios, collections of the work done by novice teachers that employers use to evaluate them. This is certainly borrowed from the arts. Take also the most *avant-garde* methods of assessing a student's progress, in which the child is evaluated on the basis of actual performance of various tasks rather than with paper-and-pencil tests. This, too, has an expressive-arts orientation. Eisner's performing-artist idea also fits well with the concept of a learning community. Teachers are like musicians in an orchestra, each making different contributions at different times, yet each following the same musical score in order to achieve symphonic sound. Consider too how good teachers function. They are much like a symphony conductor who brings out the best in a diverse group of individuals.

Autonomous Functioning

When teachers respond to the society of school by closing their classroom doors and functioning as "free agents," they tend to become parochial in their views. When autonomy is threatened, teachers tend to "close ranks" and seldom look outside their own schools or districts for answers. The flow of information to teachers and schools becomes uneven as individuals protect ideas rather than share them (Sudderth, 1987). If teachers' only claim to autonomy is their ability to make instructional decisions within the walls of their own classrooms, and if they do not work together to evolve curricular or other school-wide decisions, then teachers are alienated workers, not independent professionals (Feir, 1988).

Interactive Decision-Making

When Brophy and Good (1984) devoted thousands of hours to in-class observations, the most arresting feature of their findings was the number of decisions that teachers had to make. In fact, as Medley (1981) would argue, all areas of competence in teaching can remain inert unless they are deployed appropriately. Sound professional judgment is the essence of decision-making. Unfortunately, the concept of teachers as decision-makers is yet another misunderstood educational idea. Some administrators think that teachers will feel "empowered" if they serve on committees or select the color of their classroom walls. But teachers' disdain for "administrivia" is every bit as intense as a good administrator's. When we talk about teacher decision-making, we are really talking about *instructional* decisions, decisions that rely upon interaction with other teachers, students, parents, or school personnel. Interactive decision-making involves four steps:

1. Monitoring student behavior
2. Considering the alternatives of teacher behavior
3. Weighing the alternatives
4. Selecting a teacher behavior (Parker, 1984; Rogers, 1985)

A learning-community perspective on teacher decision-making recognizes that teachers, like other professionals, frequently want to confer with colleagues about the decisions that they have already rendered and to discuss future courses of action that they are contemplating. One startling revelation for beginning teachers is that even the experts do not have formulaic solutions to classroom situations. They come to realize that the same teacher behavior that is reasonable and effective with one child at one time may not be effective the next time with a different student or even another occasion with the same student (Clark, 1980). But, if teachers work together to improve the quality of their decision-making, then they can become "more 'flexible' teachers—teachers who can more appropriately select and reject instructional alternatives, who can better use their own behavior in ways that support student achievement" (Parker, 1984, p. 221).

Decision-Making as Moral Reasoning

Sound decision-making requires even more than interaction. It also demands that teachers deal with ethics and values. In communities of learners, we must ask these tough questions about the decisions we make:

Who benefits?

Whose interests are being served? With what effects?

What is the significance of these effects on children's lives?

To what extent do teacher decisions have a limiting or distorting effect on the opportunities open to children? (Tennyson & Strom, 1986)

Take, for example, the issue of kindergarten "readiness" testing. Many schools decide whether to accept a child into kindergarten on the basis of one brief sample of behavior taken under the worst conditions. A child is often brought to the school for the first time in his or her life, herded around through the gym, and separated from the parent. Then he or she is expected to talk to a series of strangers. Afterward, some children are categorized as "ready" or "not read" or perhaps dismissed with some dreadful euphemism such as "needs a year to grow." When working parents find out that a single measure will keep their child in private care for another year, they are justifiably angry. Consider, too, the children whose home environments are not meeting their needs, such as children who are poorly nourished or without health care, children who desperately need intellectual stimulation or who are deprived of peer-socialization experiences. Denying these children school lunches, the school nurse, and medical referrals and opportunities for learning or peer interaction only serves to underscore their deprivation. If schools answer the interactive decision-making questions honestly, it is clear that the decision to exclude these children is founded on expedience and convenience for schools rather than the needs of children and families.

Educators usually get uneasy when values, ethics, and morals are discussed in the same breath with public education. But teachers and administrators make moral decisions every day and experience the weight of those decisions. Consider the situation of a superintendent in a small school district. He came into my office before the doctoral seminar one day, obviously distraught. There was a junior high school girl in his school who was being sexually abused by her father, and this young administrator had done everything within reason to help her escape that destructive relationship. Today had been their day in court, and the judge had rendered a decision: the girl would be removed from her home, based on all the documentation that the school had provided. It seemed like a victory until he remembered that the girl had a younger sister, a sister she loved and protected from her father. When he had seen that child's stricken face, the magnitude of what would probably happen hit him. He tried imploring the judge to reconsider, but the decision was made and there was no recourse. He decided to look for a new job because, as he said, "If I find out that the sister has become the second victim, I will murder him or become suicidal." We talked about education that afternoon, about the fact that he had acted in good faith and could not blame himself for being unable to right every wrong. We talked about doing the right thing in good conscience and standing by helplessly as it becomes the wrong thing. We are talking about moral reasoning. As Tennyson and Strom (1986) point out, moral reasoning has four key elements:

- Commitment to rational thought
- Orientation to moral principles such as respect, equity, freedom
- Identification with the interests and welfare of others beyond duty or common decency (empathizing with child, parents, administrators)
- Motivation to act accordingly

More often than not, action brings re-evaluation (Tennyson & Strom, 1986). The only way to avoid this type of self-blame is to say and do nothing, which ultimately troubles us even more. One source of validation and support as we make both monumental and small decisions is the professional community.

Colleagueship

Many researchers have concluded that:

- Teachers are usually isolated from one another both physically and psychologically
- There is little in the school environment that encourages teachers to change from conventional practices
- Teachers rarely have opportunities to come together to discuss curricular and instructional concerns
- Most teachers do not feel that they receive genuine support from their fellow teachers (Goodlad, 1983; Kottkamp, Provenso & Cohn, 1986; Kerr & Zigmond, 1986; Lieberman & Miller, 1984; Rosenholtz & Kyle, 1984)

Findings such as these have led to the recommendation that schools become more collegial. But what is colleagueship? Basically, colleagues are a group of individuals who have a common goal with a vested interest in the outcome; they "are responsible for themselves, but are committed to each other" (Kraus, 1984, p. 126). Responsible colleagueship does not operate like a social club, with everyone being "nice" to everyone else. True, colleagues lend support to one another. But they also confront or censure colleagues who violate generally agreed-upon principles. Although colleagues always accept one another as people, they do not always accept the behavior of their peers. Failing to make this distinction is a serious error, one that can cause teachers to become nonsupportive, particularly of new teachers who have not yet established themselves in the organization. Nonsupportive co-workers cause trouble, instill self-doubt, socialize negatively, criticize methods, and are cold and distant (Applegate, Flora & Lasely, 1980). Conversely, supportive colleagues acknowledge efforts, cooperate to solve problems, build self-esteem, listen with a nonjudgmental ear, and invite others "into the fold" (Applegate, Flora & Lasely, 1980). Frequently, the nonsupportive colleague's motivation is to keep a shaky hold on professional self-esteem by being all-knowing and clinging to "facts." As time passes, even that hold will give way in "a world where knowledge, skills and values become obsolete more rapidly" (Benjamin, 1989, p. 9). Supportive colleagues, on the other hand, tend to be lifelong learners who always see room for improvement in themselves and who usually recognize the good in others.

The Case for Collaboration

In a synthesis of what futurists recommend, Benjamin (1989) concludes: "Collaboration, cooperation and teamwork, rather than individual achievement, will be the mark of an advancing society" (p. 9). Interdependent organizational structures are most appropriate "if the completion of one task or function hinges upon how well another task or function is performed" (Kraus, 1984, p. 100). Clearly, this is the case in schools. As evidence, consider the teachers' lounge lament: "What are they doing over there in the (fill in the blank with an earlier grade level)? These kids don't even know —!" Teachers do rely on one another to be committed to the *telos* of learning and to prepare children for what comes next, educationally speaking. This is the crux of the need for collaboration in schools: everyone has a job to do, and they can do it better through teamwork. The particular type of teamwork needed is based on small groups wherein people can get to know and trust one another. Within that group, they begin with the task and build "structures and processes around it, rather than starting with the hierarchical structure and force-fitting the task to it" (Kraus, 1984, p. 101).

School–University Partnerships

Paolo Freire (1989) tells the story of an intellectual who wished to become an advisor to a group of peasants who were working as lumberjacks in the forest. He went to them day after day until finally one of the peasants said, "Look . . . if you think you come here to teach us how to cut down a tree, it is not necessary, because we already know how to do that. What we need to know from you is whether you will be with us when the tree falls" (Shor & Freire, 1989, pp. 152–53). Whenever I hear talk about partnerships between basic education and higher education, I am reminded of Freire's parable. Such liaisons have much to recommend them, but, if they are to fulfill their promise, the university faculty must be teacher–scholars who will stand by classroom teachers when the trees fall. Unless university people are prepared to give this level of support, they succeed only in shaking a few trees, leaving teachers to rake up the debris and put the forest back in order.

Too often in school-based educational research, teachers and administrators have contact with the researcher at three points: prior to the study (e.g., to obtain permission), at the outset of the study (e.g., to gather the pretest data), and near the conclusion of the study (e.g., to gather post-test data). Usually, school personnel have little involvement in the planning phase. Study outcomes are sometimes difficult to understand without a background in statistics and even more difficult to translate into practice. Current trends in educational research and modern research methods are better grounded in real-world classroom activity. As a result, teachers' active participation in these research efforts can inform professional practice and contribute to their professional development. The important thing is that these efforts be truly collaborative and simultaneously enhance the learning of children, teachers, and researchers.

Teachers who continue to develop professionally have learned to accept responsibility for their own professional growth, to exercise sound professional judgment, and to work together in pursuit of the *telos* of learning. They fully appreciate the paradox that self-development is intertwined with contributions to the development of others. For them, self-care and caring are not competing forces. Rather, they are complementary aspects of developing human potential.

Chapter 7

FINDING OUR VOICES
AS TEACHERS

Most people believe that all that is required of teachers is knowledge of the subject matter. We know much better. We have seen many experts in the content who cannot teach. The world is full of people who can do, but can't teach. We can.
                                                                    —Albert Foshay, 1990

EIGHT YEARS AGO, I participated in a conference of the Canadian Council of Teachers of English in Montreal. That same year, I attended the International Reading Association conference in the United States. There was one startling difference. IRA publishing displays were dominated by basal reading series, and their major selling point appeared to be all of the supplemental materials — workbooks, flash cards, vocabulary charts, transparencies, and the like. The displays were colorful, elaborate, and designed to grab the attention of passersby. In Canada, the scene was dramatically different. There was exactly one rather barren table with a basal series on display, while the most numerous and popular displays were of children's literature. At lunch, I asked a group of Canadian teachers about the differences I had observed. "We had those dreary basals," one teacher said. "Yes," another offered, "but they didn't work, so we threw them out. Well, not literally — I still have a set in my room, and I use them occasionally if all else fails or a child seems interested." When I asked how they taught reading now, they looked rather surprised. Then a teacher from Montreal said, "Why, we use fine literature, of course."

Meanwhile, back at the university, I was fighting the good fight. Many of the seniors in my language-arts methods course were anxious to learn about basal readers because that was the "real world" of teaching. I contended that any self-respecting sixth-grader could read and use the teacher's manual and that, since these aspiring teachers were going to many different districts with many different programs, this focus was inefficient at best. (I did compromise a bit and give them time to browse through the various basal series in our curriculum center.) At the time, American education was focused on "burnout" and "stress," and I despaired of teachers taking on the educator's equivalent of city hall, the textbook industry. Now I look around and see a groundswell of interest in literature-based curricula. It has happened, not just in California or New York City, but at schools that are virtually inaccessible after a six-inch snowfall. This has happened, I think, because whole language is more than a buzzword or a packet of curriculum materials. In its authentic form, it is a specific type of learning community, a "scribal community" with literacy at its core (Purves, 1990).

About five years after my "contrasting conferences" experience, one of the best principals I know told me this story:

When I started as principal of this school, my kindergarten and primary grades teachers were ripe for a change. They had done all the paper-blizzard routine *ad nauseum* for themselves and the children. I read Selma Wasserman, quoted somewhere as saying, "If curriculum is the stuff of life, then life here is withered, dry and gutless." It was that way for these teachers. They felt that their classrooms were being sapped of the very things that motivated them to become teachers in the first place. My first-grade teachers, for example, regularly gave up their planning period to be outside with the children at recess. When I asked them why, they said that it was the only time they got to talk to the children informally, that the rest of the time they felt driven to drag children through the recommended work. I suggested that we meet to talk about alternatives. Five years later, we had a developmental early-childhood curriculum, one that was supported by the "Developmentally Appropriate Practice" guidelines from the National Association for the Education of Young Children. The greatest achievement of my professional career was hearing about what happened after I moved on. A new, hot-shot principal came in and started telling them that they should return to the old way of doing things, but the teachers held their ground. They informed him that they had already been down that road and had no intention of backtracking. What a transformation!

This is a good example of teachers "finding their voice." I like the voice metaphor for several reasons. First of all, it implies that we are being heard. Second, it reminds us of our singing voices, our vocal range, that place where the voice neither bottoms out on the low note nor squeaks to hit a high note. It is that place where our voices do not quaver, where they ring out loud and strong. A third reason why the analogy of the voice works so well is that, through practice, a person can extend her or his vocal range. It is, in fact, the extent of the range and the versatility within it that contribute to a vocalist's talent. Fourth, just as with the singing voice, our teacher's voice is developmental. Just as a young child begins with a vocal range of about five notes, novice teachers begin with very limited repertoires. By the time that teachers become experts, their versatility is comparable to a "trained" singing voice. Fifth, a voice is something that you possess, and developing it is an inside-out operation. No one can bequeath a voice to you or improve it for you. Rather, they can listen and encourage, offer suggestions, guide your practice, or function as role models. But you are always the one controlling your own voice. Sixth, and finally, what enables anyone to sing gloriously is a combination of talent, confidence, experience, and persistence. It helps if you have mentors, appreciative audiences, and fellow musicians; it helps if you feel like a member of the choir.

Here is how Marian Anderson (1990) describes finding her voice as a teacher:

> In situations where I followed my intuition, letting myself respond to the person, I felt confirmed, validated, liberated. When I did what was expected of me and reacted only to the situation, I felt a disloyalty to students. I wondered why I had continued to respond in ways that clearly did neither me nor the students any good. The more I thought about it, the more I saw that my reluctance to respond on a more personal level was based on fear. My inability to go with my feelings lay with my fear that I would not be considered a good teacher if I did not meet certain expectations . . . Isn't it our fear that children will fail the system that accounts for many of the practices we institute in the classroom? (p. 73)

Personal narratives enable us to express our authentic voices as teachers. The deeply felt stories of our lives in classrooms increase our ability to reflect upon teaching and to gain insight. Stories are capable, too, of encouraging us in the truest sense of that word — to take heart and to embolden. If, as Schaefer (1975) contends, we must be daring and "teach on the verge of peril" in order to be effective, the stories of teachers' lives can be a source of inspiration and strength.

The Power of Narrative

Insistence on "hard data," factual accounting, and empirical research has made us feel that our stories have little to contribute to understandings about teaching. Nothing could be further from the truth. One story about one teacher can be more instructive than an encyclopedic treatment of a subject. A fine example is Elizabeth Vance's (1990) journal about Eric, a child who has AIDS and is enrolled in her school. This personal account of professionals trying to support a dying child goes beyond mere information and illuminates the human consequences of the AIDS virus. It tells us how it was experienced. Vance's personal narrative captures the complexity of her role as principal. Her December 10 entry is about Kris, Eric's physical-education teacher. Kris has suffered an even more personal loss, and her principal writes:

> When I got to school at 7:00 this morning, I noticed that Kris was already in the gym. Suddenly, she burst into my office. She was sobbing. I took one look at her and opened my arms. I held her until she could say the words, "My little sister, Erica, was killed yesterday in a car accident. I'm here just getting ready for the sub, and then I've got to go. Her name, her name is just like Eric's." It felt like too much. Kris is six-months pregnant, she's helped every minute of the way with Eric, and now her little sister is dead. I helped her gather her things, took the plans, sent her home with her husband, and tried to begin the day (p. 8).

As this poignant episode illustrates, nothing tells us more about a person than the stories he or she chooses to tell. When I read this principal's diary, in her clear, honest voice, I felt as though I knew her. That is because personal narratives are a way of

> structuring experience itself, laying down routes into memory, for not only guiding the life narrative up to the present but directing it into the future . . . [A] life as led is inseparable from

a life as told — or, more bluntly, a life is not "how it was" but how it is interpreted, told and retold (Bruner, 1988, p. 528).

As teachers, we need to get back in touch with the belief that shining a beacon on one person's story can illuminate the lives of others.

Last summer, I worked with a group of educators who were new mentor teachers. As we stood around the coffee urns, conversation turned to memorable moments in teaching, times when it all seemed worthwhile. An administrator spoke:

> This is a story about one of the high school English teachers in our district. He would be too humble to share this, so I'll tell it about him without mentioning his real name or the student's name. There was a girl in Ron's class who was really struggling, not academically but financially. Her father had been laid off since the steel mill shut down and was doing odd jobs. Her mother worked as a waitress. They were desperately poor. In late November, the one thing they did own, a run-down house that had been in the family for years, burned to the ground. They lost every material possession in the fire, and they had no insurance. Of course, the community rallied to help them, but some things were overlooked. Ron read in this student's journal that she had saved all year to make it a really special Christmas, but now all of her gifts had been destroyed in the fire. On his commute home, he heard about a "Christmas Wish" contest on the radio. The rules were simply that the best 250-word essay explaining why a particular Christmas wish should be fulfilled would win the prize. Ron put his writing skills to work, hoping to make this unselfish young woman's Christmas a great one. His wish was for her to have money for presents for everyone in her family, a tree, a dinner, and some spending money for herself. Ron was driving home when he heard that his "Christmas Wish" had won first prize. He had to pull the car off the road because, as he said, he was crying too hard to see. Now, just to give you an idea what kind of man Ron is, he never told the girl or her family who had been their benefactor. I feel privileged that he thought enough of me to share this story. I feel honored to be considered one of his trusted colleagues.

Reflections on Teaching

In recent years, much has been written about Schon's (1983) concept of the reflective practitioner. This idea has caught both teachers' and teacher educators' imaginations because, I think, it is one of the few approaches to the study of teaching that adequately captures both its joys and its frustrations. If something goes right, we savor it; when something goes wrong, we analyze it. Where few opportunities for colleagueship exist, we turn to spouses and relatives and friends. Remain in the company of good teachers and you know stories of their students. College roommates may be overheard to ask, "So, what did _____ do today?" Spouses supply second opinions to the question teachers have already asked themselves a hundred times on the way home: "Did I do the right thing?" Sometimes a teacher's own child becomes envious of these usurpers of the parent's attention and becomes fascinated by the behavior — particularly the misbehavior — of children in a parent's class. When expert teachers reflect on educational matters such as these, they evaluate and re-evaluate their decisions, examine the situation from various perspectives, and take responsibility for their choices.

As we have seen, one thing that differentiates expert from novice practice is the number, richness, and flexibility of the "scripts" that teachers bring to the classroom setting. Research suggests that the scripts of experts from all walks of life contain highly specialized knowledge and skill which are efficiently organized by episodes, events, or cases (Carter & Doyle, 1989). In other words, we use story structures to capture the essence of what we have come to know. Through these narratives, experts are able to

> use richly elaborated conditional knowledge to interpret situations, bring a variety of information and procedures to bear on the case, and reflect constructively on their experience ...Although experts' procedures and patterns of thinking are often routinized or even automatic, their methods are not formulaic. Rather, they can adapt flexibly to a wide variety of standard and novel circumstances in their domain of expertise (Carter & Doyle, 1989, p. 61).

Last summer, a group of twenty college students worked with small groups of children under my direction. As Anita's group assembled, a four-year-old boy arrived at school for the first time in his life, literally kicking and screaming. The boy's mother was trying to calm him down and drag him in, but Tony was punching her and clinging to objects as he went by. As a former preschool and first-grade teacher, I had seen quite a few distraught children at the beginning of school. Anita tried two strategies. First, she talked about the fun they would have and invited him to join; next, she admired his shoes, hoping to distract him. Tony was having none of it. I could read Anita's mind like a tickertape: "Will I have to face this for the next six weeks? What do I do now?" I pulled over a chair and invited the mother to stay with Tony until he felt more comfortable. Her facial expression was a mixture of relief and surprise. "Everybody told me it's best just to leave them or they cry all the time," she explained. About fifteen minutes later, Tony was participating gleefully in the activity that Anita had planned, and his mother left without incident. In our seminar afterward, the prospective student teachers wanted to know how I had known what to do. I told them that you seldom *know* exactly what to do; you just learn to focus on the child's problems first. I had evaluated his violent reaction as "terror rather than tantrum," so I tried something to reassure him. As I looked around the room, I could see twenty students, many of whom would become teachers, mentally filing this story away for future use. Seymour Papert (1990) explains the use of teacher narratives this way:

> Understanding learning is my lifelong passion. I have pursued it in many ways. I have read solemn theoretical treatises. I have even made theories of my own. But interestingly I find that what helps most is not the proliferation of abstract principles. I gain more by extending my collection of "learnings" — concrete learning situations that I can use as "objects to think with" (p. ix).

Thinking about the stories of our lives as teachers is a fundamental practice of the reflective practitioner.

Types of Reflection

Schon (1988) identifies two basic types of teacher reflection. Reflection-*in*-action takes place while the incident is occurring and reflection-*on*-action takes place afterward. Two incidents experienced by Ms. Bleakney, a first-grade teacher, illustrate this useful distinction. She is conscious of the importance of "wait time" and believes that she is implementing that knowledge. Yet one day, when she asked a question, waited for a few seconds, and then called on David, he gave her an exasperated look and said, "I'm thinking!" This was reflection-in-action, because she was prompted to reconsider her "wait time" assumption at that moment and make immediate adjustments in the pace of her lesson.

For an instance of reflection-on-action, Ms. Bleakney chose this story about Artie:

> One spring morning, Artie, one of my first-graders, walked into class with a handful of daffodils and a sick look on his face. He told me that he had a stomach-ache, then asked, "Do you want to know why?" Artie had eaten three daffodils. I grabbed his hand and rushed him to the nurse's office. She called the Poison Control Center, and they assured us that daffodils were not poisonous. Artie would be fine.
>
> But why did Artie eat the daffodils in the first place? That was my next question. Artie's answer was: "One of the big kids on the bus told me he would be my friend if I ate three daffodils. So I did." I had a serious talk with Artie. I had an even more serious talk with one of the big kids on Artie's bus! Looking back on this incident reminded me of how important it is for children to feel accepted. If Artie felt it was so important to have a "big kid" for a friend that he would eat daffodils, I have to wonder about the children who seem less secure than Artie. This reinforces, in my mind, the need to create successful learning situations and to build children's sense of self-worth and acceptance.

Stories like this one and the reflections on it have the power to affect teacher behavior. Perhaps Ms. Bleakney will be more receptive to a sixth-grade colleague's suggestion that they initiate a cross-age tutoring program. Perhaps she will choose children's friendships as the topic of a paper she is assigned to write in a graduate-level child-development course. Maybe she will teach a lesson on making good judgments that includes several simulation activities and small-group discussion. Whatever the result, her story and her reflections upon it can help her to find her teacher's voice.

Signs of Progress

Finding our voices as teachers is a gradual process, but there are markers along the way that let us know we are making progress.

Three signs that the community is advancing in the direction of a learning community are:

1. *Asking why.* The people in learning communities learn to be questioners and to develop patience when dealing with complex issues. They ask themselves who they are, how they arrived there, who they can become, and how they might get there (Abbs, 1974). Perhaps most importantly, they ask, "Why?" Take, for instance, the case of parents who were called into school because their generally well-behaved daughter had instigated a "revolt" in kindergarten. The teacher reported that she had assigned a coloring page and five-year-old Shaina had said aloud, "Boring, boring." Soon the other children at her table, like penitentiary prisoners with tin cups, were taking up the chant and tapping their crayons in rhythm. Why? From everything I could determine, the children reacted in this way because it *was* boring. And why did the teacher overreact? Because she knew the children were right! If, instead of imploring the principal and parents to intercede on her behalf, the teacher had asked why, Shaina's behavior would have been an opportunity for improvement rather than a threat to authority. The "Why?" question can be the great leveler, and quality schools pose it all the time.

2. *Reducing risks.* There is no learning, no progress without risk-taking:

> The right to fail is of the essence of creativity . . . The creative act must be uninhibited and marked by supreme confidence; there can be no fear of failure — nothing inhibits so fiercely, or shrinks a vision so drastically, or pulls a dream to earth so swiftly, as fear of failure (Sullivan, 1963, p. 191).

Upitis (1990), an accomplished musician, classroom teacher, and professor, tells her story about contacting the fifth-grade teacher who instilled her love of music. Much to her former student's surprise, the now-retired teacher wrote:

> When I began teaching music, it was because there was no one else in the school willing or able to do it. I had nothing more than a love for music and song . . . Since I didn't play an instrument, it was not me but you who did the work, the learning. You were the ones who practiced, improvised, experimented, created. All I did was to set the conditions for to make that possible (p. 8).

As this teacher's story suggests, we cannot fulfill our ideals of teaching nor realize our full potential unless we reserve the right to make mistakes and learn to trust one another.

3. *Sharing successes and failures.* A student teacher whom I supervised in sixth grade read a Christmas crafts idea in a magazine. The activity involved pounding lollipops into small pieces, arranging them into clusters/shapes, surrounding the shapes with black licorice strings, and melting them in the oven to create "stained-glass pictures." When I first passed by the room, the children were flailing away. Half an hour later, they still were not close to having enough with which to make anything approximating a "stained-glass" picture and it was time for them to change classes. As I entered the room, a boy dropped a handful of lollipop sticks and candy debris into the trash can. "Here's what I think of your art project, Ms. Kowalski," he said. She could have kept her failure a secret, but instead she walked in at lunch time and announced, "Here's a project to put on your 'Never Again' list." By sharing her failure, she prevented others from making a similar mistake. In fact, her colleagues encouraged her to write to the magazine and let the editors know that the idea was impractical.

When every teacher in a building can meet with a small group of colleagues and say, without any feelings of diminished status, "I need help with. . ." there is a sense of community. The reverse is also true. When a teacher feels free to celebrate successes without fear of engendering envy, schools are headed toward an ethos of excellence.

Self-Actualization

It is common to talk of immaturity, meaning that a person is childish rather than child-like. Maturity, according to Freud (1935), is the "capacity to work and love." Most educators are also familiar with Maslow's idea of self-actualization. The term is used and people understand that it is the pinnacle of self-growth, but few understand its particulars. In his classic book *Toward a Psychology of Being,* Maslow (1968) described a number of common characteristics of the self-actualized individual. We have become self-actualized when we:

- Accept reality with all of its complexities and ambiguities
- Accept others and do not feel threatened by them
- Become sufficiently secure to be spontaneous, original, and inventive
- Focus clearly on problems without personal biases

- Become comfortable with ourselves and learn to enjoy solitude as well as social interaction
- Resist enculturation and appreciate perspectives different from our own
- Learn to enjoy life and take pleasure in the little things
- Feel a sense of spirituality and oneness with other living things in the present, past, and future
- Have a sense of unity with all human beings, yet very rich and deep personal relationships with both men and women
- Enjoy the work in achieving the goal as much as the achievement of it
- Have a constructive sense of humor which is not aimed at putting others down

Confronting Fears

Often, the thing that prevents teachers from becoming self-actualized is fear. One of the worst fears of teachers is the censure of colleagues. In business, it is common to talk of "management by walking around"; in education, it could be called "evaluation by walking around." Paradoxically, the same profession that is characterized by isolation is incredibly public where general incompetence or momentary mistakes are concerned. In the time that it takes to pass by the door, other teachers and administrators in the building make judgments about whether things are going well or not so well. The key criterion in these admittedly high-inference judgments is the amount of chaos detected or assumed. Each passerby has a personal definition for a chaotic classroom, a definition which adjusts somewhat to the teacher's years of experience. In fact, a teacher whose classroom is completely out of control is almost certain to feel shunned by colleagues who fear that chaos will infect their classrooms as well. Rather than risk this, many teachers "keep the lid on" at all times. Perhaps this is why John Goodlad's (1984) overwhelming impression after thousands of hours of observation was that American classrooms are "emotionally flat."

Every teacher knows that an out-of-control class is the biggest teaching disaster short of a major lawsuit. No matter how many new "hot topics" are presented at an inservice day, classroom management will always draw a crowd. Understandably, only the most secure and confident teachers will pursue an innovation that forces them to change, puts them on shaky ground by decreasing their control. Facing these fears is a critical stage in self-actualiza-

tion as teachers. Ira Shor and Paulo Freire (1987) have this to say
about the fears that prevent teachers from realizing their potential:

> Ira Shor: When I speak with teachers, fear is like a damp
> presence hovering in the room. I suspect that more people feel
> this fear than speak about it. It's embarrassing to admit publicly
> that what stands in the way is not only the difficulty of experi-
> menting with students but also the professional or political risks
> accompanying opposition . . . Fear comes from the dream that
> you have about the society you want to make (pp. 55–56).
>
> Paulo Freire: Yes! Fear exists in you precisely because you
> have the dream. If your dream was to preserve the status quo,
> what should you fear then? (p. 56). The more you recognize
> your fear as a consequence of your attempt to practice your
> dream, the more you learn how to put into practice your dream!
> (p. 57) . . . If you don't command your fear, you no longer risk.
> And if you don't risk, you don't create anything (p. 61).

When teachers and administrators lose the dream and stop
taking risks, they go the way of all professionals who deny their
fears. A police officer who refuses to admit fear often abuses
suspects; an emergency-room intern who quits practicing the dream
begins to view patients as the enemy; a salesperson who will not
take risks may lose even more sales by being apathetic. In psychological terms, we tend to become aggressive, defensive, or with-
drawn when we feel threatened. How does the denial of fears affect
teachers and administrators? I sat at lunch in a small town one day
and overheard the following conversation between a high school
principal and a classroom teacher:

PRINCIPAL: Did you see that black kid who just enrolled?

TEACHER: Yeah. Why is he going to school *here?*

PRINCIPAL: He's a foster kid. You should see his record. He's
been on probation three times since school started. After the social
worker finished her spiel about "starting over" and left, *I* talked to
him. I told him that if he caused any trouble in *my* school, I would
shove my fist so far down his throat that it would come out the back
of his neck.

TEACHER: Yeah, he ought to understand that — you're speaking
his language. You didn't put him in Ariel's class, did you?

PRINCIPAL: No, she's an idiot.

TEACHER: Oh, I don't think so. She's just overwhelmed by

thirty-six kids. They should really have four tenth grades instead of three. Is anyone looking at that for next year?

To me, this is an example of what happens when administrators and teachers lose their dream and avoid risks at all costs. The principal is denying his fear of loss of control and lashes out at the student; his teacher friend will not risk having high expectations for the student or disagreeing with his boss; and Ariel, a tenth-grade teacher, has evidently become apathetic because she feels powerless.

Intrapreneuring

One strategy for confronting our fears as teachers is to work inside the system for change, to function as "intrapreneurs," a term coined by Gordon Pinchot III. Most of us are familiar with entrepreneurs—individuals who strike out on their own and work outside of the organization to create some new business venture. The intrapreneur is a maverick of sorts, too. The major difference is that intrapreneurs work within the organization (Pinchot, 1985). As educators, this intrapreneurial perspective is more useful. Few of us will abandon our commitment to public education and create a school of our own. More than likely, we will need to work from inside the school to effect meaningful change. How can this be achieved?

Some strategies for changing educational organizations from "the inside out" are described below. The first three are from Shor and Freire; the remaining ideas are based on Pinchot (1985).

1. *Accumulate "deviance credits," the right to oppose by doing legitimate institutional tasks well.* If you focus exclusively on what is wrong, you will be labeled a troublemaker. It is less easy for the organization to dismiss your efforts as the rantings of a malcontent if you are competent, cooperative, and cheerful employee most of the time who actively resists some of the time. That is why it is important to choose your battles and to be alert to opportunities for change.

2. *Create an "ideological map" of the institution; i.e., figure out who is aligned with whom, on what issues, and why.* That way, when you raise an issue, you know where to begin, how direct or indirect you need to be, and how best to shepherd your idea along. Make several copies of a checklist with the names of everyone involved in making a decision in your department, school, or district. Find out what objections, if any, they might have to an idea and figure out what it would take to earn their support—and, of course, their vote.

3. *Never be alone.* An administrator once told me that his professional development strategy was not unlike his experience as a scoutmaster. "You simply gather the faculty together and say, 'Okay, who wants to be an Eagle Scout?' It's not for everybody, so you don't hold it against those who don't want to try. But, by the same token, you cannot discourage those who have the ability and desire to excel just because there are others who cannot or do not wish to join them. In a true meritocracy, everyone is invited and welcomed in, but each person is also free to decline the invitation." An important skill for teacher/intrapreneurs to develop is to figure out who can be counted on and work with colleagues whom they admire whenever possible. Even colleagues who openly oppose you can be counted on to "spread the word"; even colleagues who are lackluster will often go along with the majority.

4. *Be true to your goals, but be realistic about ways to achieve them.* The most common mistake in changing schools is to think that they can undergo sweeping changes in short order. Instead of pushing for instant transformation, create a three-year plan for reformation. One fourth-grade teacher inherited a very dated social-studies unit on careers. It was riddled with stereotypes: men were depicted as doctors, lawyers, principals, and chief executives, while women were mothers, nurses, and teachers. The two other fourth-grade teachers were happy to continue with the unit because it was familiar, so she selected the part that disturbed her the most — the sexism — and offered to change that. She involved children in creating a collage of "women at work," invited a female principal and a male kindergarten teacher to speak to the children, and used children's literature to counteract stereotypes. The second year, she worked on expanding the range of career options. One of her most successful lessons involved small groups of children in selecting a career and charting all of the people and occupations related to it. Some of the children's choices were a rock star, a wrestler, a fashion designer, and a television talk-show host. Each year, the teacher wrote down the goals achieved during the previous year and what she hoped to achieve in the year to come. In three years' time, the other two teachers were convinced that it was one of the best things they did all year and put their creative energies to work. By the third year, they were presenting their career-education curriculum at a workshop during the district's unified inservice day.

5. *Do any job needed to make your project work, regardless of your job description.* Too often, teachers give up on an idea because they do not have the help or materials. I knew two teachers

who attended a summer workshop on "hands-on science." The first complained that she could not get her school to buy her what she needed and went back to the dreary lessons in the book. The second sent a letter home asking the parents to donate inexpensive or throw-away materials that could be used to conduct experiments. She put the program into practice because she overcame the barriers instead of sitting down next to the roadblock and crying.

6. *Remember that it is easier to ask for forgiveness than to get permission.* The moment that you ask if it is okay to do something, it raises doubts. If it is a minor thing that certainly will not hurt anyone and has the potential to help someone, do it first and act contrite later if that becomes necessary. I learned this lesson early. My first year, I asked if I could create a classroom library corner with used books, a carpet, a table, and comfortable seating that I had bought at rummage sales. This request set off a chain of communication among the administrators. The major objections were that some children would have an advantage that others did not and that it would upset the custodian. After Thanksgiving, when everyone had forgotten about the request, I set up my library corner. When the principal mentioned it, I acted confused about the decision and pointed out that, every afternoon, I put the chairs up and rolled up the carpet so that the custodian would not have to. We got our library, and several other teachers followed suit.

7. *Work underground at the beginning to avoid triggering the organization's "immune mechanism."* Too much publicity too early can quash a project. Wait until things are running smoothly and there are results to share. Otherwise, those who are striving to protect the *status quo* may deflate your trial balloon before it has a chance to get airborne. The added advantage of this approach is that it disarms habitual complainers who suddenly feel that they are "behind the times." Their reaction, quite predictably, is, "When did all this happen?" You can respond cheerfully with the equivalent of, "Where have you been?"

8. *Remember to thank mentors, sponsors, and colleagues for their support.* If we as teachers feel unappreciated by the general public, that is no reason for teachers to disregard those who support them. Over the years, I have helped many teachers and administrators who are doctoral students to publish their work. Although the manuscripts begin in a course, the real work of getting them into print typically takes place on my own time long after the course is over. Usually, I read these manuscripts ten or twelve times, and often I am more of a co-author than an editor. It

interests me to see how these novice writers respond to my efforts. Some students have insisted that I be listed as a co-author, some have included an acknowledgement with the published manuscript, some have written a thank-you note or sent me flowers, and nearly all send me a copy of the published work for my files. A few act as if they were victimized by some ritualistic form of editorial hazing. Ironically, those who have been more generous tend to continue to write and become increasingly independent, while those who were less gracious have, to a person, ceased writing. Being ungracious, it seems to me, has even more serious consequences for the recipient of support than it does for the giver.

9. *Avoid the "mortgage mentality"—come to work each day willing to be fired.* Too many teachers paint themselves into imaginary corners. They can teach for 25 years and never even see a colleague fired, yet they fret about losing their jobs all the time. I had a conversation with a colleague recently about a controversial issue, and he said: "I don't think you should expect untenured faculty to take a stand. Leave it to the tenured full professors. They have more job security." I was musing over the fallacy that conviction is a seniority-linked trait when another colleague retorted, "You're wasting that argument on Mary. She was just as outspoken as a new assistant professor as she is today. If anything, she's mellowed!" Confidence comes from competence, not seniority. This is one reason why you should never be afraid to let others know about the successes of the learners in your classes. When they know and you know that you are a good teacher, you can afford to be more outspoken and assertive.

As teachers lead the way in making the transition from bureaucracy to community, they must keep in mind:

> We teachers can help other people learn. That is our function in the world. However, teaching requires specialized knowledge. We have it, most people don't. We, for example, know the difference between teaching and telling. We know what is implied by the phrase "you learn what you do." You don't learn what is presented to you; you learn your response to what is presented. We know how to turn what would otherwise be a random experience into a learning experience (Foshay, 1990, p. 31).

Every craft, every profession, begins with teaching and depends on teaching for its continuance. When teachers accept the full magnitude of that simple fact, they will no longer be heard to say, "I'm just a teacher." Teaching is a fundamental function in every social group in every culture around the world. It is through the interaction of the less experienced with the more experienced — however informal or formal — that we communicate about the past, focus on the present, and shape the future. When we express pride and confidence about our unique talents as teachers, we have found our professional voices. It is then and only then that the *telos* of learning, our primary purpose, will prevail.

REFERENCES

Abbs, P. (1974). *Autobiography in Education*. London: Heinemann.

Anderson, M. (1990). "Creating a Climate of Affirmation: Education Beyond Fear." In J. M. Newman (ed.), *Finding Our Own Way* (pp. 73–76). Portsmouth, N.H.: Heinemann.

Applegate, J. H.; V. R. Flora, and T. J. Lasley (1980). "New Teachers Seek Support: Some People Are Supportive and Others Aren't." *Educational Leadership* 38:74–76.

Arends, R. I. (1983). "Beginning Teachers as Learners." *Journal of Educational Research* 76:235–42.

Bent, E. (1990). "Who Should Have Control?" In J. M. Newman (ed.), *Finding Our Own Way* (pp. 56–70). Portsmouth, N.H.: Heinemann.

Boucher, C., and S. Weinstein (1985). "Training Professionals to Be Powerful and Collaborative." *Contemporary Education* 56:130–36.

Bloom, A. (1987). *The Closing of the American Mind*. New York: Simon & Schuster.

Britton, J. (1988). In M. Lightfoot and Nancy Martin (eds.), *The Word for Teaching Is Learning: Essays for James Britton*. Portsmouth, N.H.: Heinemann.

Brophy, J. E., and T. L. Good (1984). *Looking in Classrooms*. New York: Harper & Row.

Bruner, J. S. (1988). "Research Currents: Life as Narrative." *Language Arts* 65:574–83.

Callahan, R. E. (1962). *Education and the Cult of Efficiency*. Chicago: University of Chicago.

Carter, K., and W. Doyle (1989). "Classroom Research as a Resource for the Graduate Preparation of Teachers." In A. E. Woolfolk (ed.), *Research Perspectives on the Graduate Preparation of Teachers* (pp. 51–68). Englewood Cliffs, N.J.: Prentice-Hall.

Clark, C. M. (1980). "Choice of a Model for Research on Teacher Thinking." *Journal of Curriculum Studies* 12:1:41–47.

Clark, C. M., and P. L. Peterson (1986). "Teachers' Thought Processes." In M. C. Wittrock (ed.), *Handbook of Research on Teaching* (3rd ed., pp. 255–95). New York: Macmillan.

Clark, C. M., and R. J. Yinger (1977). "Research on Teacher Thinking." *Curriculum Inquiry* 7:4:270–304.

Cohen, E. G. (1990). "Continuing to Cooperate: Prerequisites for Persistence." *Phi Delta Kappan* 72:2:134–36, 138.

Combs, A. W. (1988). "New Assumptions for Educational Reform." *Educational Leadership* 45:38–40.

Combs, A. W., and D. C. Avila (1985). *Helping Relationships: Basic Concepts for the Helping Professions.* Boston: Allyn & Bacon.

Coopersmith, S. (1981). *The Antecedents of Self-Esteem.* Palo Alto, Calif.: Consulting Psychologists Press.

Cross, K. P. (1981). *Adults as Learners.* San Francisco: Jossey-Bass.

Cullum, A. (1971). *The Geranium on the Windowsill Just Died, But Teacher You Went Right On.* New York: Harlin Quist.

Dale, E. (1984). *The Educator's Quotebook.* Bloomington, Ind.: Phi Delta Kappa.

Darling-Hammond, L. (1987, January). "The Requirements and Benefits of Responsible Professionalism." Paper presented at the Holmes Group Inaugural Meeting, Washington, D.C.

Darling-Hammond, L. (1984, January). "Mad Hatter Tests of Good Teaching." *The New York Times,* January 8, p. 57.

Dembo, M. H., and S. Gibson (1986). "Teachers' Sense of Efficacy." *Education Digest* 51:35.

DeVries, R., and L. Kohlberg (1990). *Constructivist Early Childhood Education: Overview and Comparison with Other Programs.* Washington, D.C.: National Association for the Education of Young Children.

Dewey, J. (1938). *Experience and Education.* New York: Collier.

Dewing, A. S. (1954). "An Introduction to the Use of Cases." In M. P. McNair (ed.), *The Case Method of the Harvard Business School.* New York: McGraw-Hill.

Dodd, A. W., and E. Rosenbaum (1986). "Learning Communities for Curriculum and Staff Development." *Phi Delta Kappan* 67:523–25.

Duckworth, E. (1986). "Teaching as Research." *Harvard Educational Review* 36:4:481–95.

Duckworth, E. (1972). "The Having of Wonderful Ideas." *Harvard Educational Review* 42:2:217-32.

Editorial Statement, Editors of the *Journal of Curriculum Theorizing* (1990). Quoted in A. Miel, "Bringing Honor to the Teaching Profession," in M. Kysilka (ed.), *Honor in Teaching: Reflections* (p. 12). West Lafayette, Ind.: Kappa Delta Pi.

Eisner, E. (1985). *The Educational Imagination.* New York: Macmillan.

Eisner, E. (1988). "The Ecology of School Improvement." *Educational Leadership* 45:24-29.

Eisner, E. (1990). "Who Decides What Schools Teach?" *Phi Delta Kappan* 71:523-25.

Emig, J. (1981). "Non—Magical Thinking: Presenting Writing Developmentally in Schools." IN C. Fredericksen and H. Domenic (eds.), *Writing: The Nature, Development and Teaching of Written Communication* (Vol. 2). Hillsdale, N.J.: Lawrence Erlhaum Associates.

Erikson, E. (1950). *Childhood and Society.* New York: W. W. Norton.

Evans, E., and M. Tribble (1986). "Perceived Teaching Problems, Self-Efficacy, and Commitment to Teaching among Preservice Teachers." *Journal of Educational Research* 70:81-85.

Fagan, M. M., and G. Walter (1983). "Mentoring among Teachers." *Education Digest* 49:51-53.

Feinman-Nemser, S., and M. Buchmann (1987). "When Is Student Teaching Teacher Education?" *Teaching and Teacher Education* 3:255-73.

Feir, R. E. (1988). "The Structure of School: Teachers and Authority." ERIC Document Reproduction Service No. ED 257 806.

Fennimore, B. S. (1989). *Child Advocacy for Early Childhood Educators.* New York: Teachers College Press.

Foshay, A. W. (1990). "Let's Teach!" In M. Kysilka (ed.), *Honor in Teaching: Reflections* (pp. 24-34). West Lafayette, Ind.: Kappa Delta Pi.

Fosnot, C. T. (1989). *Enquiring Teachers, Enquiring Learners: A Constructivist Approach.* New York: Teachers College Press.

Freeman, E. B., and J. A. Hatch (1987). "Emergent Literacy: Reconceptualizing Kindergarten Practice." *Childhood Education* 66:21-24.

Freir, P. (1972). *Pedagogy of the Oppressed.* New York: Herder.

Fullan, M. (1982). *The Meaning of Educational Change.* New York: Teachers College Press.

Fuller, F. (1969). "Concerns of Teachers: A Developmental Conceptualization." *American Educational Research Journal* 6:207-26.

Fuller, F., and O. Bown (1975). "Becoming a Teacher." In K. Ryan (ed.), *The 74th Yearbook of the National Society for the Study of Education* (Part 2). Chicago: University of Chicago Press.

Futrell, M. H. (1989). "Mission Not Accomplished: Education Reform in Retrospect." *Phi Delta Kappan* 71:8-14.

Gage, N. L., and D. C. Berliner (1989). "Nurturing the Critical, Practical and Artistic Thinking of Teachers." *Phi Delta Kappan* 71:212-14.

Gardner, H. (1983). *Frames of Mind: The Theory of Multiple Intelligences.* New York: Basic Books.

Gehrke, N., and R. Kay (1984). "The Socialization of Beginning Teachers Through Mentor-Protégé Relationships." *Journal of Teacher Education* 35:21:24.

Glasser, W. H. (1990). "The Quality School. *Phi Delta Kappan* 71:425-35.

Glover, M. K. (1990). "A Bag of Hair: American First Graders Experience Japan." *Childhood Education* 66:155-59.

Goodlad, J. I. (1987). "Toward a Healthy Ecosystem." In J. I. Goodlad (ed.), *The Ecology of School Renewal* (pp. 210-21). Chicago: National Society for the Study of Education.

Goodlad, J. I. (1984). *A Place Called School: Prospects for the Future.* New York: McGraw-Hill.

Goodlad, J. I. (1983). "A Study of Schooling: Some Implications for School Imrovement." *Phi Delta Kappan* 64:552-58.

Hallinger, P., and J. Murphy (1985). "Characteristics of Highly Effective Elementary School Reading Programs." *Educational Leadership* 42:39-42.

Harper's Magazine (1986, February). "How Not to Fix the Schools." No. 272, p. 39.

Heath, D. (1986). "Developing Teachers, Not Just Technique." In 1986 ASCD Yearbook, *Improving Teaching* (pp. 1-14). Alexandria, Va.: The Association for Supervision and Curriculum Development.

Henson, K. T. (1987). "Strategies for Overcoming Barriers to Educational Change." *NASSP Bulletin* 71:497:125-27.

Hillman, C. B. (1988). *Teaching Four-Year-Olds: A Personal Journey.* Bloomington, Ind.: Phi Delta Kappa.

Hoffman, S., and L. L. Lamme (1989). *Learning from the Inside Out: The Expressive Arts.* Wheaton, Md.: Association for Childhood Education International.

Howe, H. (1983). "Education Moves to Center Stage: An Overview of Recent Studies." *Phi Delta Kappan* 65:167–72.

Hoy, W. E., and A. E. Woolfolk (1989). "Supervising Student Teachers." In A. E. Woolfolk (ed.), *Research Perspectives on the Graduate Preparation of Teachers* (pp. 108-31). Englewood Cliffs, N.J.: Prentice-Hall.

Jalongo, M. R. (1986). "Decisions That Effect Teachers' Professional Development." *Childhood Education* 42:351–56.

Jalongo, M. R. (1988). "Mentors, Master Teachers and Teacher Induction." In G. F. Roberson and M. A. Johnson (eds.), *Leaders in Education: Their Views on Controversial Issues* (pp. 88-96). Lanham, Md.: University Press of America.

Jonquiere, H. P. (1990). "My Beliefs about Teaching." *Childhood Education* 66:291–92.

Joyce, B.; K. R. Howey, and S. I. Yarger (1976). *Inservice Teacher Education.* Palo Alto, Calif.: Stanford Center for Research and Development in Teaching.

Joyce, B.; C. Murphy, B. Showers, and J. Murphy (1989). "School Renewal as Cultural Change." *Educational Leadership* 47:70–77.

Kamii, C. (1988). "Autonomy or Heteronomy? Our Choices of Goals." In G. F. Roberson and M. A. Johnson (eds.), *Leaders in Education: Their Views on Controversial Issues* (pp. 99-104). Lanham, Md.: University Press of America.

Kagan, S. L. (1989). "Early Care and Education: Beyond the Schoolhouse Doors." *Phi Delta Kappan* 71:107–12.

Katz, L. (1988). *Early Childhood Education: What Research Tells Us.* Bloomington, Ind.: Phi Delta Kappa. (Fastback #280)

Katz, L., and S. C. Chard (1989). *Engaging Children's Minds: The Project Approach.* Norwood, N.J.: Ablex.

Keizer, G. (1988). *No Place But There: A Teacher's Vocation in a Rural Community.* New York: Penguin.

Kidder, T. (1989). *Among Schoolchildren.* New York: Avon.

Kilpatrick, W. H. (1918). "The Project Method." *Teachers College Record* 19:319–35.

Knowles, M. (1975). *Self-Directed Learning: A Guide for Learners and Teachers.* New York: Cambridge.

Koehler, V. (1985). "Research on Preservice Teacher Education." *Journal of Teacher Education* 36:23–30.

Kottkamp, R. B.; E. F. Provenso, Jr., and M. M. Cohn (1986).

"Stability and Change in a Profession: Two Decades of Teacher Attitudes." *Phi Delta Kappan* 67:559–67.

Kraus, W. A. (1984). *Collaboration in Organization: Alternatives to Hierarchy.* New York: Human Sciences Press.

Lanier, J., and P. Cusik (1985). "An Oath for Professional Educators." *Phi Delta Kappan* 66:711–12.

Langer, J. A., and A. Applebee (1986). "Reading and Writing Instruction: Toward a Theory of Teaching and Learning." *Review of Research in Education* 13:171–94.

Lieberman, A., and L. Miller (1984). "The Social Realities of Teaching." In *Teachers: Their World, Their Work* (pp. 1–16). Alexandria, Va.: Association for Supervision and Curriculum Development.

Maeroff, G. I. (1988). *The Empowerment of Teachers.* New York: Teachers College Press.

Maslow, A. (1968). *Toward a Psychology of Being* (2nd ed.). New York: Van Nostrand.

McKenzie, J. A. (1990). "An Educational Safari." *Phi Delta Kappan* 72:156.

McLaren, P. (1986). *Schooling as Ritual Performance: Towards a Political Economy of Educational Symbols and Gestures.* London: Routlege & Kegan Paul.

McLaughlin, M. W.; R. S. Pfeifer, D. Swanson-Owens, and S. Yee (1986). "Why Teachers Won't Teach." *Phi Delta Kappan* 67: 420–26.

McLaughlin, M., and D. Marsh (1978). "Staff Development and School Change." *Teachers College Record* 80:69–94.

Medley, D. M. (1981). "Training Teachers to Be Decision-Makers." Paper presented at the Annual Meeting of the American Educational Research Association, Los Angeles.

Moffett, J. (1981). *Coming on Center: English Education in Evolution.* Upper Montclair, N.J.: Boynton/Cook.

Moffett, K. L.; J. St. John, and J. A. Isken (1987). "Training and Coaching Beginning Teachers: An Antidote to Reality Shock." *Educational Leadership* 44:34–36.

Moore, R. W. (1984). *Master Teachers.* Bloomington, Ind.: Phi Delta Kappa. (Fastback #201)

Moyer, J. (1986). "Child Development as a Base for Decision Making. *Childhood Education* 62:325–29.

Oakes, J. (1985). *Keeping Track: How Schools Structure Inequality.* New Haven, Conn.: Yale University Press.

Ornstein, A. C. (1981). "The Trend Toward Increased Professionalism for Teachers." *Phi Delta Kappan* 63:196–98.

Palmer, A. F. (1984). In E. Dale (compiler), *Educator's Quote Book*. Bloomington, Ind.: Phi Delta Kappa.

Papert, S. (1990). In Foreword to R. Upitis, *This Too Is Music*. Portsmouth, N.H.: Heinemann.

Parker, W. C. (1984). "Developing Teachers' Decision-Making." *Journal of Experimental Education* 52:220–26.

Peters, T., and R. N. Waterman (1982). *In Search of Excellence: Lessons from America's Best Run Companies*. New York: Harper & Row.

Pinchot, G. (1985). *Intrapreneuring: Why You Don't Have to Leave the Corporation to Become an Entrepreneur*. New York: Harper & Row.

Purves, A. (1990). *The Scribal Society*. New York: Longman.

Ralston, C. (1990). *The Effectiveness of the California Mentor Teacher Program in Retaining Quality Teachers in Classrooms*. Unpublished doctoral dissertation, Indiana University of Pennsylvania.

Raywid, M. A. (1990). "The Evolving Effort to Improve Schools: Pseudo-Reform, Incremental Reform, and Restructuring." *Phi Delta Kappan* 72:139–43.

Reeves, C. K., and R. Kazelskis (1985). "Concerns of Preservice and Inservice Teachers." *Journal of Educational Research* 78:267–71.

Richardson-Koehler, V. (1987). *Educator's Handbook: A Research Perspective*. New York: Longman.

Roettger, D. (1978). "Reading Attitudes and the Estes Scale." Paper presented at the Twenty-Third Convention of the International Reading Association, Houston, Texas.

Rogers, C. (1985). *Freedom to Learn for the Eighties*. Columbus, Ohio: Merrill.

Rogers, C. (1969). *Freedom to Learn*. Columbus, Ohio: Merrill.

Rogers, V. (1989). "Assessing the Curriculum Experienced by Children." *Phi Delta Kappan* 70:714–18.

Rosenholtz, S. J., and S. J. Kyle (1984). "Teacher Isolation: Barrier to Professionalism." *American Educator* 8:10–15.

Rubin, L. (1985). *Artistry in Teaching*. New York: Random House.

Ryan, K. (1986). *The Induction of New Teachers*. Bloomington, Ind.: Phi Delta Kappa. (Fastback #237)

Sacken, D. (1988). "A Cautionary Tale of the Ed.D." *UCEA Review* 29:10.

Saltis, J. (1986). "Teaching Professional Ethics." *Journal of Teacher Education* 37:2–4.

Schon, D. (1983). *The Reflective Practitioner.* London: Temple Smith.

Seeman, M. (1959). "On the Meaning of Alienation." *American Sociological Review* 24:783–91.

Schafer, R. M. (1975). *The Rhinoceros in the Classroom.* Toronto: Universal Edition.

Shor, I., and P. Freire (1987). *A Pedagogy for Liberation: Dialogues on Transforming Education.* South Hadley, Mass.: Bergin & Garvey.

Short, K. G. (1990). "Creating a Community of Learners." In K. G. Short and K. M. Pierce, *Talking about Books: Creating Literate Communities* (pp. 33–52). Portsmouth, N.H.: Heinemann.

Shulman, L. S. (1986). "Those Who Understand: Knowledge Growth in Teaching." *Education Researcher* 19:4–14.

Silvern, S. (1988). "Continuity/Discontinuity Between Home and Early Childhood Education Environments." *Elementary School Journal* 84:147–59.

Sizer, T. (1985, May). *Testimony Before the California Commission on the Teaching Profession.* Orange, Calif.: Chapman College.

Slavin, R. E. (1989). "PET and the Pendulum: Faddism in Education and How to Stop It." *Phi Delta Kappan* 70:752–58.

Stake, R. E. (1978). "The Case Study Method in Social Inquiry." *Educational Researcher* 7:5–8.

Sullivan, A. J. (1963). "The Right to Fail: Creativity versus Conservatism." *Journal of Higher Education* 34:4:191–95.

Swick, K. J., and M. L. Hanes (1987). *The Developing Teacher.* Champaign, Ill.: Stripes.

Sykes, G. (1983). "Contradictions, Ironies, and Promises Unfulfilled: A Contemporary Account of the Status of Teaching." *Phi Delta Kappan* 65:87–93.

Tennyson, W., and S. Strom (1986). "Beyond Professional Standards: Developing Responsibleness." *Journal of Counseling and Development* 64:298–302.

Tetenbaum, T. J., and T. A. Mulkeen (1986). "Computers as an Agent for Educational Change." *Computers in the Schools* 2:4:91–103.

Trist, E. (1976). "Toward a Postindustrial Culture." In M.

Dunnette (ed.), *Handbook of Industrial, Land and Organizational Psychology* (pp. 1011–1033). Chicago: Rand McNally.

Trumbull, D. (1986). "Practitioner Knowledge: An Examination of the Artistry in Teaching." *Journal of Educational Thought* 20:3:113–24.

Tye, K., and B. Tye (1984). "Teacher Isolation and School Reform." *Phi Delta Kappan* 65:319–22.

Vance, E. (1990). "A Tree for Eric." *The Educational Forum* 54:3:293–315.

Ward, B. A. (1984). "Do You Think of Yourself as a Teacher-Researcher? You Should!" *American Educator* 8:38–41.

Watson, B., and R. Konicek (1990). "Teaching for Conceptual Change: Confronting Children's Experience." *Phi Delta Kappan* 71:680–85.

Webster, T. (1990). "Projects as Curriculum: Under What Conditions?" *Childhood Education* 67:2–3.

Weinstein, C. S. (1989). "Case Studies of Extended Teacher Preparation." In A. E. Woolfolk (ed.), *Research Perspectives on the Graduate Preparation of Teachers* (pp. 30–50). Englewood Cliffs, N.J.: Prentice-Hall.

Wells, G. (1990). "Creating the Conditions to Encourage Literate Thinking." *Educational Leadership* 47:13–17.

Wood, F. H.; S. R. Thompson, and F. Russell (1981). "Designing Effective Staff Development Programs." In B. Dillon-Peterson (ed.), *Staff Development / Organization Development*. Alexandria, Va.: Association for Supervision and Curriculum Development.

Yinger, R. (1986). "Balancing the Art and Technics of Teaching: Renewing the Profession." *NASSP Bulletin* 70:491:75–80.

ABOUT THE AUTHOR

I DECIDED to become a teacher the first week of kindergarten, when my teacher, Miss Klingensmith, did all the right things to help me adjust. I graduated from University of Detroit-Mercy in English and Spanish, then had the opportunity to earn my teaching certificate and Master of Arts in Teaching at Oakland University. As a Teacher Corps intern, I worked with migrant and inner-city elementary school children and taught preschool during the summer. I taught first grade for three years in rural Ohio, then went to the University of Toledo, where my graduate assistantship and instructorship consisted of teaching preschool in the demonstration school and working with prospective teachers. In 1978, I earned my Ph.D. in early-childhood education and was hired by Indiana University of Pennsylvania, where I am happy to remain as a professor in the Professional Studies in Education Department.

I usually teach graduate and field-based undergraduate courses in human development, language arts, and creativity. I also teach a doctoral seminar on writing for publication. I write frequently for professional journals, among them *Childhood Education, PTA Today, The Reading Teacher,* and *Young Children.* Some achievements of which I am particularly proud are being named Outstanding Young Woman for the State of Pennsylvania, receiving the "Best Essay" award from the Association for Higher Education, being a Professional Development Institute leader for Phi Delta Kappa, receiving an Educational Press of America award for excellence in educational journalism, and being named to *Who's Who in U.S. Writers, Editors and Poets.*

In 1988, I published *Young Children and Picture Books: Literature from Infancy Through Age Six* with the National Association for the Education of Young Children. Scheduled to be published in 1991 are a college-level textbook, *The Early Childhood*

Language Arts (Allyn & Bacon), a Phi Delta Kappa fastback entitled *Strategies for Developing Children's Listening Skills,* and a chapter in a National Education Association book on multicultural education. My current project is co-authoring a college textbook on children's creativity and play for Macmillan.

I live in the hills of Pennsylvania with my husband and my dog. We bought our first house two years ago. I just knew it was a good place to write.

—M.R.J.

About *Creating Learning Communities* and the National Educational Service

The mission of the National Educational Service is to provide tested and proven resources that help those who work with youth create safe and caring schools, agencies, and communities where all children succeed. *Creating Learning Communities* is just one of many resources and staff development opportunities NES provides that focus on building a community circle of caring. If you have any questions, comments, articles, manuscripts, or youth art you would like us to consider for publication, please contact us at the address below. Or visit our website at:

www.nesonline.com

Staff Development Opportunities Include:

Improving Schools through Quality Leadership
Integrating Technology Effectively
Creating Professional Learning Communities
Building Cultural Bridges
Discipline with Dignity
Ensuring Safe Schools
Managing Disruptive Behavior
Reclaiming Youth At Risk
Working with Today's Families

National Educational Service
304 W. Kirkwood Avenue, Suite 2
Bloomington, IN 47404-5132
(812) 336-7700
(800) 733-6786 (toll-free number)
FAX (812) 336-7790
e-mail: nes@nesonline.com
www.nesonline.com